A Teacher's Guide for

Explaining Reform Judaism

prepared by

Naomi Patz and Kerry Olitzky

January, 1987

Dearest Mom —

I LOVE YOU!!!

D1710687

Behrman House, Inc.

ISBN: 0-87441-436-9

MANUFACTURED IN THE UNITED STATES OF AMERICA

Contents

Using this Teacher's Guide

Explaining Reform Judaism is a textbook devoted more to ideas than facts. The book presents the teacher with a natural two-part focus: It is necessary to give students a certain amount of historical background and overlay, thus determining one aspect of the preliminary lesson plan for many chapters; there are also many questions raised in the text that lend themselves directly to class discussion. This teacher's guide is, in effect, designed along the lines of Torah exegesis—*p'shat, derash, remez* and *sod*. For the most part, we have left the *p'shat*—the plain sense of the text—to your discretion. We make suggestions for drawing out longer explanations and explications, the *derash,* and offer discussion topics and projects for aspects of Reform Judaism that are merely hinted at in the book. This is the *remez.* It is even possible that you may occasionally wonder how we got to a particular topic from the material offered by the text. These inclusions qualify as the *sod*—the esoteric level—which you may interpret as you wish.

This guide is almost completely self-contained. Virtually all of the material needed to teach this course in Reform Judaism is contained either here or in *Explaining Reform Judaism.* The course is designed to be a classroom course; that is, the core of the subject matter will be studied in class and does not depend on extensive home preparation. Nevertheless, "classroom" is used as a generic term here, and the *Guide* can be easily adapted for informal learning experiences. In addition, each chapter contains suggestions for activities to do at home. These are all *enhancement* activities, not part of the basic course of study.

This *Teacher's Guide* is divided into parts and chapters that correspond to the parts and chapters in *Explaining Reform Judaism.* We begin each part with an introduction, which we call FOCUS. At this point we introduce a CONTEST, which we hope will provide a fun and challenging way to pique students' interest in the material. There is a contest for each of the five parts of the text; please see CONTEST #1 for more details.

Each chapter also begins with a FOCUS section, the purpose of which is to direct you to the salient points of each chapter; and a section called APPROACHES, which provides some general ideas for teaching it. Following each APPROACHES section are QUESTIONS FOR DISCUSSION and CLASSROOM ENRICHMENT. The latter section includes activities designed to augment the material presented in the student textbook.

Also appearing in every chapter (except the last two) is a section called BIOGRAPHY NOTEBOOK, which will introduce the students to important personalities in the development of Reform Judaism. Each student should be responsible for at least one biographical report during the course. They will find research sources in the synagogue library—some of the most useful are listed in the bibliography at the end of this *Guide.*

Each BIOGRAPHY NOTEBOOK section suggests specific people whose careers or ideas are in some way connected to the theme of the chapter; however, you might want to make all biography assignments at the beginning of the course to give students enough time to prepare their reports. To facilitate these assignments, turn to the Biography Notebook Assignment Record at the end of this *Guide*. There you will find a list of the personalities in the order that we suggest you assign them, plus space for you to write the name of the student responsible for that report. Following the list is Capsule Biographies, a series of short biographical paragraphs provided for your own reference.

Students should be encouraged to present their findings both orally and in writing. The written entries can be compiled into a notebook as the course proceeds. At the end of the course, reproduce the notebook and distribute a copy to every member of the class. It will serve as a collective record of their classroom experiences and their own development as future leaders of the Reform movement.

The final section of each chapter is THINGS TO DO AT HOME, supplemental activities for students to do by themselves or with parents and other members of the family. (However, the primary emphasis of the *Guide* is, as we have stated, on classroom instruction and experience.)

Obviously, it is not necessary—nor even desirable—to incorporate all the ideas suggested here into your planning. You will feel more comfortable with some than with others; the composition of your student population will help determine certain approaches. Looking at what we propose will also stimulate you to devise your own ideas for classroom implementation of the text.

Throughout the *Guide,* we refer to "your" synagogue. We mean the one in which you are teaching the course. In some cases, it may not be your own congregation, which of course gives you useful examples whenever the text or *Teacher's Guide* calls for comparisons between different synagogues and communities.

Because Reform Judaism is always in the process of evaluation and growth (*Reform,* not *Reformed*), this course has unlimited potential. As you proceed, include current new developments. This will add immediacy and heightened relevance to your course. Reform Judaism is a positive response to an ever-changing, ever-growing world. It is our prayer that we, and our students, will continue to grow in tandem with it.

Beginning the Course

It is important that you clearly indicate at the very beginning of the course that this textbook stresses ideas rather than facts. *Explaining Reform Judaism* is unusual and special because of this emphasis. Students are probably more accustomed to studying from books that require them to memorize facts about people, places and dates. We want our students to think—to think about Reform Judaism and to think about why they are Reform Jews.

Begin the course by distributing the textbook and allowing the students a few minutes to flip through it. Ask them to look at the pictures and to read the table of contents.

Part 1
What Makes Reform Jews Special?

FOCUS

Begin the class's study of this section by reading page 1 of the text aloud to the class or by having a student read the page aloud. Ask students to articulate the questions raised by the authors (in paragraph 4), and write them on the blackboard or on a large sheet of paper (which you will then tape to the wall). Don't attempt to answer the questions yet. Instead, assign each question to a student (and make a note of the student's name and the question in the appropriate place in your lesson plan or your copy of the textbook). It will be that student's responsibility to let the class know when his/her question has been answered during your study of the material. (Remember to remind the students periodically of their obligation, and to "call the question" at the end of the unit if the student has not voluntarily responded at the proper time.)

CONTEST #1

At the beginning of each section of *Explaining Reform Judaism,* a contest should be announced. Students should have as many weeks as the section is studied to prepare their entries. You can determine how the entries will be judged, if at all. Successful entries should be posted on the bulletin board (inside or outside the classroom) and, if feasible, published in the synagogue's newsletter.

The theme of the first contest is limericks. The subject matter is very broad—anything that helps explain and show the development of the Reform movement is acceptable. Here are two samples to inspire student creativity:

Zunz was the name of the man
who found out when sermons began.
Through the study of history,
he cleared up the mystery:
"Tis midrash! Now please lift the ban."

A banker in an old town called Seesen
Said "Jews, come listen to reason!"
Let's have girls study with boys,
Shorter services, less noise!"
And they found his reforms fairly pleasin'.

1

A New Movement Modernizes Judaism

FOCUS ON THE CHAPTER

Chapter One begins with a discussion of the enforced ghettoization of Jews in Western Europe, and the ways in which Jews were restricted in almost every area of life. Since there was little opportunity for them to interface with the outside world, Jews set up their own legal and social society, a microcosm of the outside world, within the confines of the ghetto.

At the end of the eighteenth century, the people of France rebelled against their government, a repressive monarchy. The French Revolution (1789) created a new form of government, the principles of which were expressed by the Declaration of the Rights of Man. "Men are born and remain free and equal in rights," it stated, and provided for freedom of speech, press and religion. It extended to all citizens the right to liberty, property and security. These rights of citizenship were also given (not without hesitation) to the Jews. However, citizenship came with a price—the Jews were told to give up their ethnic and national identity. "Everything to the Jew as an individual; nothing to the Jews as a community." For the first time in history, Judaism became *voluntary*.

The extension of the rights of citizenship to everyone became known as the Emancipation. It soon spread to other places in Europe. In Germany, a group of prosperous Jews, most of whom were merchants who had business dealings with Christians, were inspired by the potential of freedom. They wanted to take full advantage of the civil rights that were being extended to them (more slowly, granted, than in France). They rebelled against the ghetto structure and what were now, in effect, restrictions against moving out into general society.

One individual, Israel Jacobson, initiated programs that modernized worship services, gave women an active role in religious life, and helped Jews cope with being both Jewish and modern. His efforts marked the beginning of Reform Judaism.

APPROACHES

Begin this chapter by asking your students to look at the illustrations and their captions. Since these provide a kind of visual outline of the chapter, outline Chapter One using the pictures as the major headings of the outline. Then, with the help of the students, use the text material between the pictures to fill in specifics and historical details. In order to further encourage the class to read this material, ask them leading questions that will require reading the chapter (or major sections of it) to find the answers. For Chapter One, these questions might include: What would it be like to have actually lived in the ghetto? What was the French Revolution all about? What kinds of changes did Israel Jacobson introduce into Judaism?

QUESTIONS FOR DISCUSSION

1. At the beginning of Chapter One, the text says that many activities were illegal for Jews 200 years ago. Before (or after) having students read the chapter, ask them to suggest things they think (or know) were forbidden to Jews. Are there restrictions that limit Jews today in America? In other countries? (The situation of Jews in the Soviet Union and the changes in their conditions will be useful examples.) Raise such issues as quota systems for jobs, admission to universities and specialized training, private social clubs. Explain how even quotas designed for positive purposes, such as affirmative action, can be both good and bad. These were created to bring members of minority groups quickly into higher academic and better work situations, but the practical result is that they often limit places available for Jews. What suggestions do students have?

2. Expanding on pages 2-4 of the text, give students a sense of what it was like to live in a Jewish quarter or ghetto (business restrictions; educational limitations; congestion; the claustrophobia that comes from bans on travel and ignorance of new developments in science and culture, changes in clothing styles, musical tastes; and so on). Compare this to the situation of your students today.

3. After reading the descriptions of the kinds of trades and professions prohibited to Jews, have your students imagine themselves as young adults in the ghetto. How would they make a living? What would they do if they were prevented from getting proper education for entering certain professions? Include jobs they indicate that they themselves might like to do someday and also the fields and types of business of their parents.

4. Look at the anti-Semitic cartoon on page 5, and invite students' reactions. (The Encyclopedia Judaica contains some vivid examples.) Discuss the anti-Semitic *stereotypes* revealed by these cartoons. Explain how anti-Semitic stereotypes were exploited in Europe during pre-modern times to make Jews scapegoats—in order to deflect public wrath at the government, or popular fears in times of plague or during an unsuccessful war, for example, or when powerful people who had borrowed money from Jews and could not repay it used anti-Semitism as a means of getting rid of their problem. Show how the desperate situation of some midwestern American farmers in the mid-1980s has created racist organizations that blame the Jews of the U.S. for their troubles and spout vile anti-Semitic statements and threats. Be prepared for students to relate incidents that have happened to them, and help them analyze what happened. Often these are isolated and essentially harmless happenings, more the result of malicious ignorance than anti-Semitism. However, if a situation is revealed that is potentially serious, someone from your local Federation's Community Relations Council (CRC) or the Anti-Defamation League should be alerted and (if circumstances warrant it) invited to address the class.

5. Analyze with the class the reasons why some Jews were afraid to leave the ghetto and begin to exercise their freedom. Use the example of an animal or bird that, having always lived in captivity, is suddenly uncaged. Would the creature immediately escape?

6. The early Reformers felt that it no longer was necessary to mourn the loss of the Temple in Jerusalem. The possibilities inherent in full citizenship and their desire to be modern made the reinstitution of a priestly sacrificial system seem anachronistic. They therefore

removed the prayers that longed for the rebuilding of the Temple and the restoration of the sacrifices. They made other symbolic gestures as well. Discuss why (as on pages 7-9 of the text) Jacobson's synagogue was called a "temple." After all, until the early years of Reform, the word "Temple" *always* referred to the ancient Temple in Jerusalem, destroyed in 70 C.E. What was the philosophical impact of such a name change?

7. Establishing a Western style of synagogue decorum rather than an Eastern one was an important concern for the early Reformers, as the text notes on page 7. Discuss the notion that what is appropriate decorum for one place is incorrect in a different situation. Consider using as examples your classroom (possibly in contrast to other teachers' practices) and the difference between watching a film in a movie theater and watching a movie at home on television. Then apply this to the synagogue. Evaluate the positive and negative aspects of the decorum appropriate there.

8. What made Jacobson's idea of having girls join with boys at the school in Seesen so revolutionary? Do students see any advantages to having students separated by sex in school, as was the case in Europe and still exists in certain elite private schools around our country as well as in some yeshivot?

9. Expand on the reasons why the changes in decorum and style that Jacobson made were radical departures from the pattern of worship of his day. Would we consider his changes—using musical instruments at worship services, shortening the liturgy—radical today? Are there *any* changes in worship services that we might consider overly radical? Chances are, since all breaks with what people are comfortable with become "radical" to the people who are accustomed to them, almost *anything* could be a radical departure! However, you can come up with some extremes—a rock music band and laser show, drive-in worship with speakers attached to the windows of cars, etc. Also, to relate the concept of such changes to the students' interests, use examples from school scheduling (major shift in class hours or vacation time, for example), or the rules for a well-known playground or board game.

10. Why was confirmation introduced in the Reform movement (at the expense of bar mitzvah)? What is its relationship to the Protestant ceremony of confirmation? Is the confirmation ceremony in your congregation like the one in Berlin in 1817? How is it different? What has been retained/rejected/changed? How does your course of studies for confirmation compare to the earliest confirmation preparations?

11. Ask your students to talk about Shabbat evening services at your synagogue. Help them identify "beautifying" aspects of the service. How might they change the service to make it more "beautiful" and more "satisfying"? Use pages 6-7 of the text for help.

CLASSROOM ENRICHMENT

1. Without giving any explanation, require some of your students (by whatever designation you choose—eye color, those wearing sneakers, etc.) to wear a distinguishing symbol (a yellow badge, a paper dunce cap, etc.) during the class. Consider restricting them to one part of the classroom, making them do additional things to get recognized to speak, or denying them something everyone else is getting. Shortly before the end of the session, process their feelings. Then relate these feelings to the laws forcing Jews to wear special

clothes, shoes or badges (as described on page 2 and pictured on page 4). If you wish to show additional examples of "Jews' clothing," see Alfred Reuben's *Book of Jewish Costume.*

2. Have students debate this statement: "Resolved, the confirmation ceremony shall *replace* bar/bat mitzvah."

3. As an experiment in making reforms, invite two students to devise a plan for "reforming" your classroom. Allow them to implement change. Ask another student to record their triumphs and defeats—and the new problems and discontents their changes create. Relate their experiences to Jacobson's innovations.

BIOGRAPHY NOTEBOOK

Make a biography notebook for the classroom that can either be added to during the course of the year or be available for reference as needed. It should contain information on important people in the development of Reform Judaism, beginning with this chapter's entries **Israel Jacobson** and **Moses Mendelssohn.** Capsule biographical entries on each suggested figure appear at the end of the *Teacher's Guide.* Assign one student responsibility for each biography. Oral presentations could be made, a classroom reference book created, or copies of all the reports could be reproduced and collated for student reference.

THINGS TO DO AT HOME

1. Chapter One serves as an introduction to the modern Jewish situation, with its focus on the results of the French Revolution and the accomplishments of Napoleon. Ask a student to prepare a brief report on Napoleon's Sanhedrin and present his/her findings to the class.

2. Ask a number of students to research the history of confirmation and bar/bat mitzvah in your synagogue. Suggest that they talk to the rabbi and also to some "old timers." Let them present their findings to the class. Have there been changes? What caused them? Is the current situation best? Will there be other changes in the future? Should there be? Have the entire class ask their parents if they became a bar/bat mizvah and/or were confirmed, and to describe the ceremony. Some of the parents may have photographs, invitations, etc. they can share. How do the parents compare *their* experience(s) with what is done today? Ask your students to compare their parents' experiences with what was done in Israel Jacobson's time.

3. Make a list of the changes in Reform Judaism that appear in Chapter One. Then have students interview extended family members and friends, including those who belong to other movements. Do they agree with the innovations of Reform? Which ones? Why/why not?

2
A Revolutionary Idea

FOCUS ON THE CHAPTER

The central emphasis of this chapter is the discovery by Leopold Zunz that midrashim historically served the role sermons do today. For a number of centuries prior to his time, sermons had been delivered only twice a year. But at private services in Berlin, held at the home of a merchant named Jacob Herz Beer, Zunz and others preached regularly. The traditional Jewish community leadership objected vehemently to these Reform services, and particularly to the information that Zunz and others were providing in their sermons. The community leadership was so frightened about what the reformers might do to Judaism that they complained to the King of Prussia. The king, who had his own political reasons for opposing innovation of any kind, declared it illegal to hold private services and illegal to introduce any changes into the service.

Zunz turned to scholarship as the best means of countering the ban. He researched the development of midrash literature over the centuries and documented its homiletic role in Jewish life. His scholarly discovery validated his contention that sermons were not a modern innovation and that it was legitimate to preach every Shabbat. His research methods became a paradigm for other scholars who were looking to establish Jewish precedents for seeming innovations.

Zunz's "detective work" in establishing his case for sermons is fascinating, and some of it should be conveyed to the class. No one before him had ever done a history of a Jewish practice or idea. Indeed, no one had ever looked at Judaism as if it had a history that could be studied. No real Jewish encyclopedias existed, and no Jewish history books. The volumes of midrashim themselves seldom gave the names of their authors, when they were written or even in what country. In fact, the people who wrote them occasionally claimed that they were actually written many centuries earlier by one or another great teacher. The authors of the Midrash weren't interested in historical accuracy. They were explaining Jewish tradition, not analyzing it.

Yet analyzing was exactly what Zunz needed to do. Before he could write a history, he had to be able to put his evidence in chronological order. This enormous research job took years. Finally, Zunz was able to assign dates and places and fix the sequence of the midrash books. Now he could give a proper history of Jewish preaching.

Chapter Two of the text ends with the statement that the publication of Darwin's theory of evolution confirmed for Reform Jews their certainty that Judaism, like other aspects of life, changes (evolves) over time.

APPROACHES

Introduce this chapter to the class by playing the role of Leopold Zunz. Explain how you were prevented by law from preaching to the congregation. Describe to the students "your" method of scholarship (as per page 12). Tell the class why you feel that Jewish leaders fought the idea of change (see page 14), and conclude with a brief declaration of your feeling that you are in the right (based on Darwin).

QUESTIONS FOR DISCUSSION

1. How did Leopold Zunz prove that giving sermons was not a Reform innovation but had always been an integral part of Judaism? In what way were midrashim key to the development of the sermon in Judaism? What is the role of the sermon in the synagogue today? What is the practice in your congregation? Is a sermon preached every week? If not, what takes its place?

2. Share with your students an example of a midrash on a biblical narrative that they are already familiar with from Religious School studies. By analyzing these stories and how they have been developed to expand and explain the text, you can show your students how the midrashic process works. The Midrash Rabbah series published by Soncino Press, or Louis Ginsberg's *Legends of the Jews,* published by the Jewish Publication Society, are your best sources for these midrashim.

3. If change is an indispensable part of Judaism, as the authors imply in Chapter Two, then ask your students to imagine the kinds of changes taking place in the world by the year 2050. Will traditional Judaism have to change with the world? Will Reform Judaism be prepared to respond?

4. In Europe, each community had its own synagogue, which was supported through a broad, general tax assessment. The synagogue had enormous control over the lives of the Jews in that community. Do your students like that idea? Would they prefer one congregation for the whole community, with financial support shared among all the Jews—or do they prefer the system we have here, which permits not only a choice of affiliation but also whether or not to affiliate at all.

5. The leadership of the organized Jewish community of Berlin complained to the King of Prussia in 1823 about the services being held in the Beer Temple. Under what circumstances might an organized group of Jews today complain to government authorities about other Jews? Has this ever happened in America? *Could* it happen in America? How do your students think the government would respond?

CLASSROOM ENRICHMENT

1. Invite the rabbi to class in order to discuss how he/she decides on appropriate topics for sermons. Have the class decide which sermons (if any) might have been considered proper for sermons before Israel Jacobson's innovations and how these sermons relate to Zunz's discovery of midrash-as-sermon. Also ask the rabbi to talk to your students about how Moses reacted to the kinds of changes implied in the text on the bottom of page 14. Is the very process of change and development an inherent part of Judaism?

2. Zunz considered the sermon to be an old Jewish custom; his opponents opposed his position. Have the class develop a set of criteria to determine what they believe can be

considered Jewish. Test it against the practices of your synagogue. How do individual students relate to/identify with these criteria? Are there things the students have designated as "Jewish" that do not apply to or have been rejected by the synagogue? By the students and/or their families? What does this demonstrate about Reform Judaism?

BIOGRAPHY NOTEBOOK

For the biography notebook, assign a student responsibility for the life of **Leopold Zunz.** Have him/her consider what qualified Zunz for his self-imposed assignment. How did it happen that he had the vision and courage to take on the Prussian government and, in the process, revolutionize our way of studying and understanding Judaism?

Abraham Geiger was a leading spokesman for Reform Judaism in Europe. He is best remembered for the controversy that followed his appointment as assistant to Rabbi Solomon Tiktin in Breslau. Tiktin was opposed to all of Geiger's ideas for the reformulation of Judaism. Since this chapter is concerned with some of the early revolutionary ideas of Reform Judaism, have another student prepare a report on Geiger for the biography notebook.

THINGS TO DO AT HOME

1. Have students work in teams to research the history of the congregation. Logical sources of information include the rabbi and executive director, old temple bulletins and ad journals, veteran members of the congregation, the dates various ritual objects were dedicated, photograph albums and other archives. The goal should be to find out how many changes in ritual have occurred over the years. This will help students appreciate how much change actually occurs over the lifespan of a congregation.

3
Reform Comes to America

FOCUS ON THE CHAPTER

Although Reform Judaism was born in Germany, it really took hold in America, where the political and social climate were from the very beginning based upon the concepts of "liberty, equality and the pursuit of happiness." This is the main concern of Chapter Three. It begins with the two great waves of 19th century immigration. The first was from Western European countries, primarily Germany, in the 1840s. These immigrants had benefited from the Emancipation while they were still in Europe. They were very different from the huge numbers of Eastern European Jews who arrived in the United States between 1880 and 1924. Reform Judaism, by this time, had developed a clearly non-traditional style with a very western flavor. Abbreviated services were conducted in English; the congregation worshiped bareheaded; mixed choirs and instrumental music were common. The Eastern European Jewish immigrants were, for the most part, shocked not only by these externals of Reform worship but also by the Reform approach to Jewish scholarship and by theological matters such as belief in the messiah. The controversy over the question of messianism is epitomized by Rabbi Isaac Mayer Wise's altercation in Albany, New York (1850) and his subsequent departure for Cincinnati. Chapter Three concludes with a look at the *Union Prayer Book,* which was very radical in its day.

APPROACHES

This chapter should be introduced by using two parallel time lines and a map. On the first time line, pinpoint the history of Jewish immigration from Europe. Show the major points of emigration on the map. The second time line should follow the early development of Reform Judaism in America, utilizing the dates provided in the text. Ask students to provide the information by reading through the chapter and suggesting names and dates.

QUESTIONS FOR DISCUSSION

1. On page 23, the text quotes an early leader of the Reform congregation in Charleston, South Carolina. What is the meaning of his statement, "This country is our Palestine, this city our Jerusalem, this house of God our Temple"? What are its ramifications? Why would the members of the Reformed Society of Israelites have liked that statement—and what reasons might your students have to object to it?

2. Talk with your class about the waves of Eastern European immigration to the United States and explain the cultural differences between Eastern and Western European Jews. How were the Eastern European immigrants different from earlier immigrants? How were

the differences reflected in the way they observed Judaism? What was their reaction to the Reform movement? In that context, it is easy to see how the Conservative movement became important in the early years of the twentieth century as the "Reform" of Eastern European Jewry in America.

3. The reaction of traditional Jews to the Reform practice of not wearing head covering at services was a very emotional one. Discuss with your students the possibility that this highly charged issue tainted the reactions of the traditionalists to every change the Reformers made. Some of these changes, in reality more significant, were visually and physically less overt and did not come in for the same kind of vehement and vociferous condemnation. Is it possible that some of these changes would have quietly been introduced into traditional worship services if everyone hadn't been so hysterical over the matter of kippot? For example, consider the shortening of the introductory prayers on Shabbat morning and other such changes described in the text. What is the practice regarding head covering in your congregation? Has this always been the case?

4. As the text describes, musaf was introduced as a supplementary service to parallel and reflect the additional sacrifices that had been offered up in the Temple in Jerusalem on Shabbat and festivals. Musaf is primarily a repetition of prayers from the morning service, with sacrificial prayers added. Discuss why the Reformers felt that both reasons— repetition and sacrifice—made musaf undesirable and prompted them to eliminate musaf from the liturgy of the Reform movement.

5. The religious calendar of modern Israel has dropped the additional days of festivals, with the exception of Rosh Hashanah which continues to be observed there for two days. This corresponds to the majority Reform practice. The Reform movement dropped the extra days that were added as a kind of protection for the festivals in the time before a fixed calendar was introduced. The "extra" days guaranteed that everyone would be observing the holidays at the proper time. What do Conservative and Orthodox congregations do? Does it matter that as a result of the Reform approach to the lunar calendar Simhat Torah is celebrated by Reform Jews on a different day than it is by other Jews in the Diaspora? Specifically, are there any problems with other Jews in your community or with the school system because Reform Jewish youngsters attend school on days when Orthodox and Conservative children are in synagogue? Have your students had any relevant experiences?

6. When Rabbi Isaac M. Wise came to America he wanted to create an *American* Judaism, that is, a Judaism molded by the ideals of America and modernity. He had no intention of being involved in the development of a separate movement within Judaism. Only after the founding of Hebrew Union College, in 1875, did Wise realize that his liberal approach to Judaism would not serve the needs of all American Jews. Tell your students about the early history of your synagogue. Was it founded as a distinctly *Reform* institution or was it originally intended to serve the needs of all the Jews living in the community?

CLASSROOM ENRICHMENT

1. Contrast the Jewish to the Western custom of removing hats (indoors, to honor the flag, to honor the dead). Your students may be familiar with this Western practice from watching old movies. Rabbi Jacob Z. Lauterbach wrote a well-researched, much-quoted responsum

on the wearing/not wearing of kippot. You might want to bring some of its information to the attention of your students. (You can find it in the 1928 *Yearbook* of the Central Conference of American Rabbis [Vol. XXXVIII, pages 589–603]. If neither your synagogue library nor your rabbi has a copy, write to one of the campuses of HUC-JIR and ask their library to photocopy it for you.)

2. Have the class make up a list of questions to ask the rabbi. Then choose a student or group of students to interview the rabbi. The student should inquire about the criteria used to make choices regarding prayers and services. With his/her help, the student should also find out how the emphasis on the language of worship has changed over the years (Hebrew/English/German/Yiddish/other). Were sermons always preached in English? If not, when was English introduced and what was the reaction? What percentage of the service is in Hebrew today? What percentage is in English? Have these percentages changed from earlier years and, if so, how and why? The early Reformers removed parts of the traditional service. Have the student ask the rabbi how the length of a service should be determined. Should services be longer or shorter on holidays than they are on Shabbat?

3. After your students have learned about Reform Judaism's rejection of the sacrificial system, as discussed in Chapter Three, constitute the class as a rabbinic court charged with deciding if animal sacrifices should be reinstated. Tell the class that certain groups of ultra-Orthodox Jews in Israel are actually planning for such a time. Have individual students present arguments for both sides. Vote.

4. Ask your students to compare the two versions of the *aleinu* (on page 27 of the text), focusing on the issues of particularism and universalism. Using the same method, analyze with the "grant us peace" that follows. You might also wish to show your students copies of the *Union Prayer Book* and compare it with the prayer book currently in use in your congregation. Key items of comparison would include the amount of Hebrew, the variety in the number of worship services offered, references to the Holocaust and to the modern State of Israel, the relative sexism of the language, and the "old fashioned" vs. "modern" texture of the language itself.

5. Using the model of prayers for the welfare of one's country on pages 27–28 of the text, have the class write a prayer for the United States that speaks to their dreams and hopes for this country. Try the same for the State of Israel. Then try it for a country like the Soviet Union or South Africa.

6. Invite two guests to your class—someone who came to America in one of the earlier waves of immigration and someone who came to our country recently—and ask them to talk about what brought them here and why they chose to join a Reform congregation.

BIOGRAPHY NOTEBOOK

For this chapter's entries, assign **Gustav Poznanski,** the first spiritual leader of the Reformed Society of Israelites in Charleston, South Carolina. This congregation took the first steps in developing an American Reform movement.

Poznanski's pioneering efforts were followed by other great movement builders. Foremost among them was **Rabbi Isaac Mayer Wise,** known as the "Father of Reform Judaism in America." Assign Rabbi Wise's biography to the notebook.

THINGS TO DO AT HOME

1. Have a student research and report to the class on the Geiger-Titkin controversy in Berlin (unless the topic is covered by an entry to the Biography Notebook).

2. Ask a student to find out about the beginnings of the Reformed Society of Israelites. He/she should show how the Reformed Society of Israelites in Charleston changed and grew during its first years of existence (1822–1825).

3. Assign a couple of students to trace the development of the Reform movement in your community and your congregation. During which wave of immigration was your synagogue founded? Did it begin as a Reform congregation? If not, when and why did it change? Can the influence of the early founders still be felt? In what specific ways—or things?

4. Have your students find out when their families came to America. Were they part of one of the major waves of immigration? At what point did their families choose to affiliate with Reform Judaism?

5. Ask students to discuss with their families what they think should happen during the messianic period, and the difficulty of ever realizing a messianic age. At the next session of the class, have them list the most important five events (conditions). Compare lists (i.e., messianic visions).

4
Reform Jews and Other Jews in Our Day

FOCUS ON THE CHAPTER

This chapter is about comparative Judaism. It looks at the three major movements of Judaism in North America in order to compare one to the other. The authors talk about various styles in ritual objects (such as kiddush cups and hanukkiyot) and in synagogue music. Taste in ritual objects and musical style are essentially surface distinctions, although they are often symptomatic of major differences—in attitude as well as in substance—among the movements. The textbook looks at two basic differences separating the movements: the Reform Jewish approach to conversion and the very controversial notion of patrilineal descent. This leads the discussion into Reform Judaism's problems in the State of Israel, the most distressing of which is in the area of personal status, that is, "who is a Jew?" The authors conclude the chapter by asking questions to which there are no easy answers: "How much shall we modernize? How fast shall we do it?"

APPROACHES

Introduce this chapter to your students by asking them the questions on the first paragraph of page 29. Spend some time discussing the answers to these questions. Then, together, look at the photographs of hanukkiyot on pages 29–34 as examples of the possible differences in styles of ritual objects. Give the students a few minutes to read these pages to themselves before you actually discuss the differences. In order to consider the differences in liturgical musical styles, ask a student to read page 32 aloud to the class. Then debate the two sets of issues discussed: traditional vs. modern music; solos (and choir performances) vs. congregational participation. Next, ask students to outline the process of conversion, using pages 34–36 for information or details. After they have made written outlines, ask them if they think that this approach could lead to problems for Reform Jews in the State of Israel, and why. Then tell them to read pages 36–37, to find out if they were right. Finally, discuss the questions raised in the heading of the final section of the chapter (page 38).

QUESTIONS FOR DISCUSSION:

1. You may want to precede the role playing exercise (Classroom Enrichment, #3) with a discussion about the purpose and uses of mikveh. Why was it rejected by Reform Judaism? Should it be replaced by another process, and if so, what?

2. Here is another discussion topic related to liberal Judaism and the use of a mikveh: If liberal Jews want to include traditional rituals in their patterns of observance, such as the use of mikveh for conversion, then should a liberal synagogue provide opportunities for such observances? If so, following a discussion about the use, advantages and disadvantages of the mikveh, as described in Chapter 4, have your class prepare a resolution to be brought before the synagogue's Board of Trustees to include a mikveh in any future building plans or renovations of the synagogue.

3. Discuss the resolution on patrilineal descent passed by the Central Conference of American Rabbis in 1983. It is discussed briefly on pages 35–36 of the text. What's good about it? What's bad? What are its long term positive and negative implications? Will it eventually separate Reform Judaism completely from the rest of Judaism? Will it jeopardize the Jewish future of those Jews whose Jewishness comes only from their father? What will happen when they want to get married? What will be the status of *their* children?

4. Pluralism is based on the notion that one does not have the *certainty* of truth. Orthodoxies don't have this "problem," but liberal religions (just as liberal governments) do. Discuss the subject with the class and mention the problems that arise because non-orthodoxies are so often forced into the position of being the ones to compromise (as much because they are able to as for ideological reasons). Do students describe this situation as "unfair"?

5. Jews make up only a very small percentage of the world population and we are getting to be a smaller percentage with each passing year. We all know the expression "in unity there is strength," yet there is much internal divisiveness. What if the Orthodox movement would acknowledge Reform Judaism if we agreed to halakhic conversion (mikveh with witnesses plus ritual circumcision for males), and the issuance of a *get* (a divorce document in accordance with traditional Jewish law)? Should Reform Jews give up freedom of choice and require traditional conversion for converts and *gittin* (plural of *get*) before anyone can remarry? Is it a fair price for strengthening the Jewish community, or too high a price to pay? Can the class reach a consensus on this issue?

CLASSROOM ENRICHMENT

1. Certain ritual objects will be acceptable to liberal Jews and not to traditionalists. One example is a hanukkiyah whose candle holders aren't all at the same level (the tradition requires that none, except the shammash, take precedence over any other). Bring to class two hanukkiyot that show these distinctions and show them to your students. Let the class determine what makes them different from one another (multi-level candle holders or separate shammash, as well as stylistic differences). Make clear to your students that ritual objects in modern styles and materials are not a problem for traditional Jews so long as the object itself conforms to halakhic stipulations. Since Reform Judaism has not felt bound to the halakhic strictures for ritual objects, different artistic representations in ritual objects have not been a problem for the Reform movement.

2. Many examples can be introduced to show the modernization of styles in synagogue art, architecture and ritual Judaica. Torah mantels and ark curtains provide a graphic example: traditionally, Torah mantels were covered with little lions holding up the tablets of the Ten Commandments. They were done with lots of gold thread and sequins on heavy plush

velvet. Many contemporary Jews find them old-fashioned and uninspiring. Contemporary artists and crafters have worked in many different media and textures to create original, new designs. Show the class examples of synagogue architecture and ritual Judaica over the centuries, for which many well-illustrated books are available. Don't forget the Union of American Hebrew Congregations (UAHC) film strips on art and architecture. After viewing all the examples, have the class evaluate the age and style, etc. of the ritual objects and architecture of your synagogue. If it has been redecorated, compare old and new. Which do they find more appealing?

3. Present a hypothetical situation to the class: An individual comes to the rabbi to discuss conversion. What should the rabbi say to the potential convert about why he/she should convert to Judaism? What is the process of conversion in your synagogue?

Act it out with your students. Make sure that the role playing takes into account the fact that while traditional Judaism over the years has discouraged people from converting to Judaism, the outreach program of Reform Judaism is specifically designed to make conversion to Judaism desirable and attractive. Through the role playing, elicit from your students the attitudes toward life and, perhaps, toward Judaism itself, that informs the differences in approach? What are the drawbacks of each position?

You might want to discuss a number of preliminary considerations in order to set the background for the particular role-playing situation you are establishing. For instance, does the rabbi always know the family status or background of a couple who comes to him/her to discuss getting married? How much should the rabbi ask? (Jewish tradition urges rabbis not to investigate too deeply or inquire too much! What does that suggest about the tradition? Should the rabbi try to convince the prospective non-Jewish mate to convert? If he/she isn't interested in becoming Jewish, what do members of the class think the rabbi should say and/or do next?

4. Together with the class, create a liberal conversion ceremony for Judaism. The rabbi can probably provide both traditional and liberal samples to help start the thinking process. Also consider with your students the grounds on which you might reject the request of an individual to convert to Judaism.

5. People have very strong reactions where synagogue music is concerned. Is the musical style in your congregation formal or informal? Is there a cantor, choir, organ? How would people react to alternatives? Do some regular synagogue-goers make it a point to stay away when there is a youth group service at your synagogue? Perhaps they object to contemporary music, which sounds unfamiliar to them. Does that mean that no youth group services should be held? Or that only traditional music should be played? After students have voiced their opinions on the subject, play for them some examples of different renditions (Ashkenazi, Sephardi, North African, modern Israeli, Hasidic, classical and folk) of the same prayers (ideally ones familiar to your students). How would they feel if some of these were introduced into your congregation's worship service? Would they find themselves anti-innovation and traditionalists on the subject?

BIOGRAPHY NOTEBOOK

This chapter's entry is not about a leader of the Reform movement but an early Reformer who broke away from the movement and whose ideas eventually formed the basis of a separate movement altogether. **Zacharias Frankel** is considered the spiritual father of the Conservative movement. Have a student prepare his biography for the notebook.

THINGS TO DO AT HOME

1. Ask students to look around carefully at home. What ritual objects do they find? Which are traditionally styled—or antiques—and which are products of modern artistic taste and inspiration? If possible, have students bring an example of each to class and compare them with those brought in by fellow students.

2. Assign several students to investigate the policy on conversion and Jewish status in your congregation. Their questions should deal with such considerations as, for example, how long the conversion process takes; is the ceremony public or private; is mikveh required; circumcision? Are non-Jewish spouses allowed to light Shabbat candles in the sanctuary, sit on the bimah, have an aliyah, vote or hold an office in the congregation or its affiliates? Are mixed marriages announced in the Temple flyer? Your students may think of other questions to ask as well. Have them report their findings to the class.

3. Devise a poll in class and have students sample their Jewish friends—young and old alike. How many of them follow the Reform movement's determination that personal choice should guide the kind of life they lead? Do these people consider themselves Reform Jews? If not, what is their congregational affiliation? Compare students' results. What can they learn?

4. Assignment: Write a letter to an imaginary potential convert, trying to persuade him/her to become a Jew. Be fair and deal with the possible problems he/she may face.

5
What All Jews Share

FOCUS ON THE CHAPTER

Until this point, the text has stressed the differences between Reform Judaism and the other major movements in Judaism. Chapter Five, however, focuses on what all Jews share. After a short discussion of the distinction between traditions as customs and habits, and tradition as a history of belief and practice, the text turns to a consideration of the aspects of the religious calendar and Jewish life cycle observances that are common to all Jews. With regard to historical events, the text considers the common historical memories all Jews share by virtue of being part of the same people. In our generation, the key examples are the Holocaust and the existence of a State of Israel. Finally, the authors speak of us as one big family believing in the same God, but using different ways in which to look at the Jewish world and enjoy it.

APPROACHES

The study of the material contained in this chapter should begin by presenting the class with a chart that is divided into two parts. One side should be labeled "Reform Jews"; the other, "other Jews." Go through the material in this chapter, paragraph by paragraph, with your students. Together, identify groups, ritual objects, life cycle events, holidays and historical happenings and decide on which side of the chart each belongs. Have two students act as scribes who will include each thing mentioned in its appropriate column. Don't forget to include the subjects of the photographs. When you reach the metaphor of "one family" (pages 47–48), which concludes the chapter, give your students the opportunity to explore this image fully. Is the Jewish people one family? Is it a "happy" family? Encourage students to use their own families as examples to consider if the metaphor works. Can brothers and sisters care deeply about one another yet get into arguments? Can they continue to love one another, speak on the phone, get together occasionally and still lead entirely different life styles? Draw the implications for world Jewry, and even for the divisions within the local community.

QUESTIONS FOR DISCUSSION

1. After reading the chapter entitled "What All Jews Share," ask your students to name things all Jews share and have someone record the suggestions. Is the list a long one? Are your students different from the other Jewish youngsters in the community? If so, in what ways? If not, what does this teach us?

2. Using the information in Chapter Five as a guide, and perhaps consulting the relevant

articles in the *Encyclopedia Judaica* and/or appropriate issues of *Keeping Posted,* discuss the basic philosophical differences separating the various movements in Judaism (Reform, Conservatism, Orthodoxy and Reconstructionism). When the class has a sense of the distinctive elements of each movement, ask them if they think that Jews should try to become more like one another? How would they go about accomplishing that?

3. Using a dictionary, give the class definitions of the words *ritual, tradition* and *custom.* Discuss what makes one different from another. Does your congregation have any special customs or traditions? How did they come into being?

4. Beginning on page 43, Chapter Five suggests ways in which we share common historical memories. What does that mean? What common historical memories do your students share? How many that they recall can be identified as Jewish? Have each student who makes a proposal come forward and write his/her individual response on the blackboard. Then move on to another aspect of common historical memory. Present the metaphysical concept that everyone was at Sinai to receive the Torah, as described in the text. Who agrees? Who disagrees? Why? Ask students why they think that our history teaches that humanity began with the creation of a single human being. (Fascinatingly, scientific discoveries about genetic heritage may support that idea! What your are looking for here, however, is not a scientific answer but an ethical one—"we are all one family.")

CLASSROOM ENRICHMENT

1. The authors emphasize that Reform Judaism is a Judaism of choice, that is, Reform Jews choose what we wish to observe rather than follow doctrines and dictates established by our ancestors. Involve your students in a exercise of choice. Write the names of individual Jewish events (holidays, life cycle, ritual observances) on large sheets of paper (or on different sections of the board) and tack them up on the classroom walls. Have students "sign up" for all the events in which they participate. Are these choices of conscious intent (observances they have chosen to do—or chosen not to do) or omissions made by neglect (things their families have never done because they weren't aware that such practices existed or had never been exposed to them)?

2. We continue to establish new traditions in Reform Judaism, as did the early Reformers. Can the class name some new traditions—secular or Jewish? Start with American traditions. Martin Luther King Day is a good contemporary tradition on a national scale. So is the new custom of moving national holidays to the nearest Monday rather than celebrating them, as used to be done, on the actual date of their occurrence. What about Jewish traditions? What traditions do you have in your classroom? Divide the class into groups and ask each group of students to "create" a tradition for the class. How do they propose to implement it? How will they make it appealing enough for the rest of the class to want to make it their own? A follow-up discussion to this exercise may well elicit the understanding that for the most part traditions emerge in response to needs or evolve with shifting tastes and styles; few lasting traditions are externally imposed.

   As an exercise in testing this last idea, have the class create a new bar/bat mitzvah ceremony. Let them invent as many new "traditions" as they want. Send the ceremony to the rabbi and solicit his/her response.

3. Create a checklist of all the things your students did in preparation for bar/bat mitzvah.

Did every student do the exact same preparation as every other? Next to this checklist, put the known bar/bat mitzvah preparation requirements at local Conservative and Orthodox synagogues and at a nearby Reform congregation. (Students can be assigned to find this information out from their friends.) Compare and contrast the findings. Are there more dissimilarities or similarities? More than between various students within the class?

BIOGRAPHY NOTEBOOK

Assign **Rabbi Stephen S. Wise**, another of the movement's greatest leaders, who stressed the concepts of Jewish peoplehood and unity in both his pulpit and organizational activities.

THINGS TO DO AT HOME

1. Ask parents (or students) to prepare a number of traditional foods from different Jewish cultures and bring them to class for a "taste" of the variety of Jewish tradition. They could also (or alternately) compile a mini-cookbook of these recipes, which could be distributed not only to your class but to the rest of the religious school and possibly even to the entire congregation.

2. Have students use the *Encyclopedia Judaica* to find out how many different movements there are in Judaism, and then write a one-line description of each. In order to do this efficiently, assign one major or fringe movement each to several students, who will bring their one-liners to class for discussion, comparison and listing.

3. Assign each student to make a list with his/her family of the special family traditions in which they participate—the kind that may have been passed from one generation to another or the kind they've developed together (who sits where at the table, what they do on birthdays or Hanukkah or Thanksgiving or on the day they come home from camp, among other possible examples). Invent a "new" tradition and ask your students to introduce it at home this Shabbat at dinner. Have your students evaluate its impact on members of the family. Did they enjoy it? Did it move them? Did they feel stupid doing it? Is it something they would like to continue doing? As a result of their experience with this new "tradition," do they feel that "traditions" can be successfully invented and imposed? If not, ask them to explain how traditions come about.

4. Design an individual project for each student that brings to life the concept of "Jews helping Jews." The project should be ongoing and should last for a meaningful duration of time. In class, or on an individual basis, evaluate the practical and emotional results of each project. Examples might include visiting senior citizens at home, where they can be helped with small household tasks, or in a nursing home; helping out at a rehabilitation center; volunteering to work with the physically or emotionally impaired; collecting money for Jewish causes; adopting a Soviet Jewish family and writing to them, and about them to the president and members of Congress; working as a volunteer in the synagogue library— and any other Jewish social service project that helps an individual, the synagogue or the community as a whole. (But be careful: Some young people are exceedingly uncomfortable in nursing home/senior citizen center/hospital environments, and imposing such a project on them might have negative rather than positive results.)

5. Assuming that a choice of synagogues is available in your immediate geographic area, request that students attend services at an Orthodox congregation, a Conservative congregation and a Reform congregation (ideally, if your students are familiar with the service at your own synagogue, then they should also visit another temple for purposes of comparison). Afterwards, initiate reports on these visits leading to class discussion.

Part 2
Who Tells Reform Jews What to Do and Believe?

FOCUS

This part of *Explaining Reform Judaism* is concerned expressly with the authority structure in Reform Judaism. If Reform Jews do not accept God as the direct source of the Torah and God, therefore, did not give the commandments, then the individual Reform Jew must make decisions for him/herself about what to believe and how to practice Judaism. The focus of this section of the book is on the individual as the decision-maker in Reform Judaism.

As you did with the focus on Part One, read the page that introduces the section (page 49) aloud to the class, or ask a student to do so. Again assign each of the questions (in paragraph 2) to an individual student and request that the students call attention to the fact that the question is being answered when the appropriate subject is discussed in class.

CONTEST #2

In this contest, the object is to imagine the most desirable state of freedom—and then provide the twist of realization (the reality factor) that of necessity limits the freedom. For example:

I can't imagine anything more wonderful than not having to get up every day to go to work. Realization: I'd starve to death.

If I could choose to do whatever I wanted, I'd spend all my time in the swimming pool. Realization: I'd look like a prune.

If I were really free, I'd never go to sleep. Realization: yawn, yawn, yawn.

6
The Reform Jewish Emphasis on Personal Freedom

FOCUS ON THE CHAPTER

This chapter is built around the pivotal point in the philosophy of Reform Judaism, the Reform emphasis on personal freedom. As such, it is probably the most important chapter in the textbook. The chapter begins by exploring how, as people get older, both their freedom of action and their responsibility for their behavior and decisions becomes more and more up to them. They grow less dependent on their parents and more dependent on themselves. As background, the text gives a historical overview, very briefly contrasting the times when people were not free with the opportunities that have come with democratic society. Continuing the theme of freedom that was initially presented in Chapter One (on page 4), the textbook explains how the spirit of democracy, applied to Judaism, creates liberal Judaism. A discussion of the advantages—and the disadvantages—of freedom concludes this chapter.

APPROACHES

Begin class consideration of the chapter by giving the various dictionary definitions for the word ''freedom.'' Review the introduction to the chapter and present, in your own words, the scenario of the freedom/responsibility balance involved in growing up. Introduce the next section, ''Why Were People Less Free Before?'' by raising a discussion about freedom. Lead students to deal with the directed questions that are included in the textbook, such as ''How can anyone be against liberty?'' After talking about the desirability of freedom, and the restraints bullies, tyrants, legal systems and society place upon freedom (moving from the most negative, intrusive limitations to those which permit the orderly functioning of life), ask students to write (and perhaps diagram) why they think it was so important to the early Reformers that they be able to ride on Shabbat. To help them formulate an educated answer, ask them to read the section called ''The Democratic Spirit Gives Rise to Reform Judaism'' (pages 53–55). Finally, make two columns on the board (or on large sheets of paper tacked to the wall). Label one column ADVANTAGES and the other PROBLEMS. Encourage students to brainstorm the advantages and the problems that come with Jewish freedom, with one student serving as the recorder for each column. Make sure that all of the items in the final section of Chapter Six are covered in this discussion.

QUESTIONS FOR DISCUSSION

1. The beginning of Chapter Six concerns the increasing amount of freedom parents give

their children as the children grow older. Do your students think they had much freedom when they were young children? How much has it increased as they have grown older? Imagine with them the amount of freedom they will have as adults. Get your students to talk about personal freedom vis-a-vis parental authority and the imposition of guidelines, standards and restrictions. How do they deal with the problem? Do they talk back, or try to explain their own position? Do they say they'll agree and secretly disobey? Or do they give in and do whatever their parents want? These responses, which reflect a situation with which they are familiar, can be drawn upon to help understand the relationship of Reform Judaism to traditional Judaism, and of democracy vis-a-vis totalitarianism.

2. Based on the information offered on page 51 of the text, ask the class if they think that people would *choose* totalitarianism? Yet it happens today. Provide them with a current example of an oppressive totalitarian regime that nevertheless has loyal adherents and defenders. Explore the reasons why a totalitarian system has its appeal. (You might want to look at *Escape From Freedom,* by Erich Fromm, for the classic treatment of this idea.)

3. Compare the traditional notion of Torah as revealed by God to the description of the Reform notion of Torah (on page 53 of the text).

4. Review the laws prohibiting driving on Shabbat (as described on pages 54–55), and discuss their ramifications today. Have students assess the advantages gained by driving on Shabbat, as well as the disadvantages.

CLASSROOM ENRICHMENT

1. In order to take the freedom of choice seriously, good Reform Jews, according to the authors, must be well educated Jews. To help the class understand this concept, have students try to play a game they have never seen, or ask them to revise the rules of an unfamiliar game—without giving them the rules. Will the result be a revised game, a totally different game or chaos? Ask the class to give some examples of how Reform Jews might use the tradition as a guide for making decisions about observance.

2. Many aspects of programming and religious services in the synagogue are based on personal freedom. For one thing, people can choose whether or not to participate. Have students think about the synagogue and come up with suggestions for ways to add even more freedoms. Ask them to voice their suggestions to the class so that students can compare ideas and evaluate them. Perhaps the class could agree on one suggestion to present (in writing or in person) to the appropriate officer of the congregation for possible implementation.

BIOGRAPHY NOTEBOOK

Rabbi David Einhorn, an important figure in the early Reform movement, was known not only for his influential prayer book, *Olath Tamid,* but also for his strong and public opposition to slavery. As this chapter discusses questions relating to democracy and freedom, now is an appropriate time to assign Einhorn's biography.

THINGS TO DO AT HOME

1. Ask your students to imagine that they are responsible for setting limits for a younger brother or sister. How would they go about doing it? After some class discussion on the subject, ask them to raise the matter with their parents; how do their parents come up with guidelines for them, as they grow up? If your student is the eldest child, are his/her parents strictest with him/her? Do they let younger sibling(s) do things your student wasn't allowed to do—or had to wait to do? If the student is a younger sister/brother, is the opposite true? Do the parents agree with this assessment?

7
Changing Times and the Changes in Reform Judaism

FOCUS ON THE CHAPTER

This chapter takes us back to the drastic change forced upon our people by the destruction of the center of Jewish religious life—the Temple in Jerusalem—in 70 C.E. Synagogues became the new centers of life for Jews. As with the change necessitated by the destruction of the Temple, the early Reformers believed that the Emancipation, too, mandated change—albeit as a positive rather than negative response to the new situation. The Reformers felt that modern Judaism should deemphasize the differences between people and, at the same time, emphasize the universal ethical ideals of modern men and women.

Their illusion (perhaps even delusion) of harmony, of a world getting ever-better, was shattered by the catastrophic events in Europe during the years 1939–1945, during which time six million Jews—almost one and a half million of them children—were murdered by the Nazis and their collaborators. And so, Reform Jews reevaluated their emphasis on "universal humankind" and shifted the movement's focus of belief and action to include a strong concern for the Jewish people. Individual Jews and individual congregations then had to try to reconcile the call to universalism with the needs inherent in Jewish particularism.

The establishment of the modern state of Israel breathed new spirit into Judaism as a whole, and Reform Jews responded (as did Jews in the other movements) with a renewed commitment to freedom, to hope and to peoplehood. As the authors point out, these commitments have led to a whole new "American" way of being Jewish—in summer camps for young people, in the Oneg Shabbat following Friday evening services, where coffee, cake and conversation emphasize the sense of Shabbat as a festival and the congregation's role as an extended family.

Chapter Seven concludes with a new challenge for modern Reform Jews. The text suggests that the Reform movement has entered a new phase of freedom, in which we are free to explore not only ways to expand the borders of acceptable Jewish behavior but also ways in which to live a fuller Jewish life.

APPROACHES

Begin this chapter by reviewing with your students the circumstances surrounding the destruction of the Temple by the Romans in 70 C.E., and the Emancipation in the 18th century. Next, ask students to read the section on page 58, entitled "Modern Changes," in order to distinguish between "freedom not-to-do" and "freedom to-do." Discuss the directions in which these freedoms led and can lead Reform Judaism.

Spend a little time discussing the idea that the Holocaust not only destroyed six million of our people but also destroyed the illusion that democracy and the great ethical ideals of the Western world were a substitute for Judaism. From this discussion, draw the conclusion that the Jewish people has come to since the Second World War, namely, our obligation to have "a concern for our group as well as for every group." Using pages 61–62 for help, determine in detail with your class how this commitment can be acted upon.

This concern has been given a positive focus, as the authors note, by the establishment of the state of Israel and its impact on the American Jewish community and Jews around the world. The events surrounding the birth of the modern state—and even the Six Day War in 1967 and the Yom Kippur War in 1973—are ancient history for your students, who tend to take the existence of Israel for granted. You may be able to use the example of the aliyah of Ethiopian Jewry (Operation Moses), which hopefully most of them have heard about, to give Israel's centrality to the Jewish people definition. Ask students to look at the photographs on pages 62–64 in the textbook and react. Do they have similar feelings when their high school football team wins a game, or the professional team for which they root?

Discuss those things which are, according to page 64, uniquely a combination of "American push and practicality with Jewish idealism and folk loyalty," and which, together, create an American Jewish style. Have students suggest things to add to the list that the text begins. Put each item on a banner labeled with an American flag and a Jewish star, and hang them around the classroom.

The conclusion to this chapter is crucial to our purpose in religious education: to foster religious growth, to encourage students to appreciate their freedom by exploring ways to live a more fully Jewish life both in and outside the synagogue. Brainstorm with your students ways in which they are willing to commit themselves to living a more fully Jewish life. Have each student identify one way he/she chooses to commit him/herself, and ask the student to write it on the board.

QUESTIONS FOR DISCUSSION

1. Explain the centrality of the sacrifice system to ancient Jewish life. Discuss the degree of dislocation that must have resulted after the destruction of the Temple and the transition from the Temple cult to synagogue worship. It may also be useful to spend some time discussing the factional and ideological separation of Sadducees and Pharisees (described in the *Encyclopedia Judaica*) and the specific changes and innovations brought about by the Pharisaic revolution. The Pharisees originated rabbis, synagogue, bet din, the system of mitzvot and a belief in afterlife, for example, and they also created the mechanism for change that makes them, in effect, the *first* reformers.

2. It will be interesting for your students to analyze why Reform rejected the binding authority of the Talmud and how the early Reformers chose not to acknowledge the Talmud as the example *par excellence* of change and adaptation on the part of our ancestors. If they had accepted its significance, would they have championed it? In their pursuit of reform and change, they found the Talmud monolithic and constricting. (They didn't understand, for instance, that by stipulating the kinds of work to be prohibited on Shabbat, the Rabbis were making all other activities licit. The Rabbis' interpretations of Scripture were *their* way of reforming what they had inherited.) Therefore, Samuel Holdheim (first rabbi of the Reform congregation in Berlin and one of the organizers of the Brunswick Rabbinical Conference of 1844) could write: "The Talmud speaks with the ideology of its own time, and for that time it was right. I speak from the higher ideology of my time, and for this age I am right." Ask your students to comment on this statement.

34

3. Discuss the difference between the freedom Reform offers for creating a personal way of religious life and the constrictions of the ghetto, as described in Chapter Seven. Review the reasons why many Jews feared participating in general society (intermarriage, loss of identity, worries about the security of Jews who functioned as individuals without the protection and guidance of the community, etc.). Are any of these fears still voiced today? It was not simply that the Jews who were afraid to become active outside the Jewish community were xenophobes or anti-social—it was much more complex. A sense of the crisis and the conflict will heighten students' understanding of the bravery of the Reformers and the degree to which their new ideas and willingness to interact in general society were truly radical departures. And it will help explain why some Reformers came to substitute universalist identification for a more particularist approach to Jewish identity.

4. Chapter Seven explains how the Holocaust shattered the early illusions about a messianic age cherished by the early Reformers, who believed that the world was getting better in every way. Explore with your students any direct impact the Holocaust has made on their lives, the life of their families, the life of the synagogue and the outlook of the local Jewish community. Include the addition of prayers and changes made in the religious school curriculum. Has Judaism *itself* changed?

5. All of the innovations that Reform Judaism has brought to American Jewry give us the opportunity to make Judaism an ongoing part of our lives in many non-traditional ways. Use the list on page 64 as a trigger for your discussion. Many American Jews wear jewelry to display their Jewish pride and identity. Do any of your students? Do any object? Why? How do they feel about comparable Christian jewelry?

6. Have students explain this statement: "The early Reformers made Judaism fit into American life; today, we are attempting to make American life fit into Judaism." Emphasize the concept that early Reformers were immigrants who were trying to make themselves at home in their new country and were eager to be accepted as Americans. The early Reformers were also still "proving themselves," still working on developing an alternative to traditional Judaism. Now that the Jewish community is comfortable here and feels fully American—and the Reform movement, while it still continues to evolve, change and grow, has taken its place as a major movement in Judaism—it is time to re-evaluate the changes made by Reform and perhaps recapture some of the Jewish ethnicity the early Reformers rejected. Is this move toward greater traditional observance taking place in your synagogue? What specific examples can you and your students cite?

CLASSROOM ENRICHMENT

After the class has read Chapter Seven, have each student write one paragraph beginning with the phrase: "The world needs Judaism because. . ." Or, "Judaism should survive in order to. . ."

Invite a speaker to talk with your students about the dangers—and the appeal—of cults.

BIOGRAPHY NOTEBOOK

As the text explains, the Holocaust shattered our illusions about messianism and destroyed most of European Jewry. Among the survivors of the Holocaust was a very special man. His name was **Leo Baeck** and he was a rabbi. During his internment at Terezin and later, when he was president of the World Union for Progessive Judaism and a teacher at Hebrew Union College-Jewish Institute of Religion, his unflagging belief and his commitment to action on behalf of his fellow Jews were a great inspiration. Have a student report on Leo Baeck for the biography notebook.

THING TO DO AT HOME

1. Have students design badges that display their liberal Jewish identity.

8

The Limits of Reform Jewish Freedom

FOCUS ON THE CHAPTER

Often, the freedom available in Reform Judaism is stressed so strongly that we overlook the need to place certain limits on that freedom. This chapter begins with the need to establish limitations, using the metaphor of a bumper car to initiate the discussion. From there the text moves directly to the most critical question: Who sets the limits once divine authority is removed from the system? What happens when each individual is left to set limits for behavior based solely on the basis of conscience?

The Torah, as the text indicates, is the preeminent resource for determining our choices. Through freedom and the guidance of Torah, each Reform Jew should develop an ongoing relationship with God, the nature of that relationship dependent upon the nature of that individual and his/her personal needs and perceptions.

APPROACHES

If you are comfortable with this approach, you might begin the class discussion of this chapter by playing bumper cars in class–or by going around the room and bumping into some of the students' desks. (Or appoint one or more students to do the same. Use this to introduce the bumper car image which introduces the theme of the chapter—the need to place limits on (Reform) Jewish freedom.

Lead students to the realization that each individual truly has ultimate responsibility for his/her decisions and choices about how to believe and practice Judaism. Yet there are also outside influences on a person's decision-making. Use mundane examples to make the point, such as which member of the family gets to use the bathroom first in the morning. Then turn to Jewish examples, such as the ones listed in the first paragraph on page 68. What would happen to the life of a congregation if the day for observing Shabbat were left to individual choice?

QUESTIONS FOR DISCUSSION

1. Which is easier, setting limits for ourselves or having someone else do it for us? (Examples can include bedtime, television and telephone privileges and parental input on the students' choice of friends.) If it is easier to have others set the limits, why are we Reform Jews so insistent about setting our own limits?

2. Ours is the strongest and oldest democracy. Yet even here anti-democratic organizations

and tendencies exist—the KKK, the American Nazi Party, etc. Should they be tolerated? What about neo-Nazi marches in Jewish neighborhoods, or Klu Klux Klan rallies in black neighborhoods? Should people be allowed to publish anti-Semitic literature in America? What is the difference between "freedom" and "license"? Who should decide? Who sets the limits?

3. Now present the class with a hypothetical sports situation in which one player on the team chooses to be individualistic and either doesn't follow the game plan or hogs the ball to get personal attention. Discuss. In that light, deal with the following considerations: the need for society to limit people's freedom; the notion that one person's freedom ends where another's begins; who sets the limits in the various areas of our lives.

4. The freedom of choice that is available to individual Reform Jews is also available to Reform rabbis. Although the movement's rabbinical leadership disapproves of rabbis who officiate at intermarriages, Reform rabbis can still choose to do so. Discuss the limits of freedom that the movement should or should not impose on rabbis.

5. On page 68, the authors speak of the range of behavior that Reform Jews might consider appropriate on Shabbat, many of which would be considered wrong by Orthodox and some Conservative Jews. Discuss with your students the meaning of the term "in the spirit of Shabbat." What sorts of activities would they consider to be in that spirit? How many would consider it legitimate to observe Shabbat on some other day of the week so long as those people choosing Wednesday, for example, used the day for "appropriate" Shabbat activities?

6. Earlier in the text, the authors talked about compromises Reform Jews may have to make for k'lal yisrael (the broad Jewish community). Is choosing to observe holidays at the same time as traditional Jews a worthwhile compromise for group solidarity? Chapter Eight talks about setting limits to freedom; should the Reform movement have—or give up—the freedom to observe Jewish holidays at different times from the days that Orthodox and Conservative Jews observe them?

7. The quotation from the Babylonian Talmud, Tractate Berakhot 40a, on page 30, says, "people are forbidden to sit down to eat until they have first fed their cattle." Ask students to interpret this in a contemporary situation. What things do they have to do before they sit down to dinner—or before they can go into their rooms for the night?

8. Ask students to name obvious controls on freedom that are designed to maintain order on the roads, such as stop signs and traffic lights. Does a red light or the word "stop" on a sign actually prohibit motion? Why, then, are they normally effective? Why does society require a legal system—laws, police, a justice system and a scale of punishments from fines through imprisonment? If Reform Jews do not consider halakhah binding, what replaces the legal force of the "stop signs" for Reform Judaism?

9. The idea presented on page 70, making one's life a life of Torah—"caring to know and knowing to care"—is a difficult task. First define Torah in the broadest possible terms. Then, after discussing with the class the meaning of the concept of living a life of Torah, ask your students how they would go about persuading people to live their lives in pursuit of Torah? Can they convince themselves?

10. What does Reb Zusya's question, on pages 70–71, really mean? Why wasn't he worried about not being like Moses? What *was* his concern? Should students have a similar concern? Is it possible to know if we are living up to our own potential?

CLASSROOM ENRICHMENT

1. Extending the automobile metaphor that appears throughout the beginning of Chapter Eight, have students design a driver's license that would authorize people to ''drive'' a ''liberal Jewish car.'' What would be the requirements for such a license? What data would they include on the license? Who should have the right to issue it? Then ask the class to adapt common road signs to fit the limitation-setting needs of Reform Judaism. For example: ''Stop signs'' for what? ''One way'' signs for what? ''Do not enter'' signs? ''Slow''? ''Children crossing''?

2. Set up a ''rules committee'' for Reform Judaism in your classroom. What rules should be made and how should they be enforced?

3. Give each student an index card and ask the class to write a definition of personal freedom. Have a number of them read their definitions aloud. Ask students if any aspects of these definitions infringe on the freedoms of other people. If so, ask them to suggest limits. How willing is the presenter to accept the suggested limitations? Now collect the cards, shuffle them and arbitrarily hand them out again. How do students react to living by someone else's definition of personal freedom?

4. Following the discussion of God in Chapter Eight, try a values whip (This technique consists of posing a question and then quickly ''whipping'' around the room from one student to another, for spontaneous answers/reactions. For more information, see Sidney Simon, et al., *Values Clarification.* New York: Hart Publishing Company, 1972.) Ask students to spend some time saying to one another, ''You remind me of God when you _____.'' Together, analyze both the responses and the reactions to having made the statements and to hearing them.

5. Put a large sheet of paper, entitled ''Treasure Map,'' on the wall. Provide students with brightly colored crayons or markers. Ask every student to enter on the ''treasure map'' one way he/she thinks it is possible to find God in this world. Suggest possibilities derived from the fifth paragraph on page 73, but also encourage students to come up with truly special moments from their own lives, which can be positive examples—birthdays, times of family closeness, sunrise, the first time they held a new baby, or negative ones such as their reactions during a time of illness or tragedy or natural disaster. The ''map'' should ultimately be filled with many ways to find the ''treasure'' which is the presence (or an understanding of) God in our lives.

BIOGRAPHY NOTEBOOK

Ask a student to prepare a short presentation on the radical changes made by **Rabbi Samuel Hirsch,** some of which are listed in Chapter Eight. Hirsch should then be entered into the biography notebook(s).

THINGS TO DO AT HOME

1. To help students understand the importance of symbols and symbolism in relation to Reform Judaism's approach to ritual, ask each student to go into his/her room at home and find all of the "treasures" they have kept. Have them try to remember what the objects remind them of and why they have kept them. Are these things precious in themselves or are they *symbols* of people and events? How many have become precious simply because the things have been in the student's possession a long time—and the original reason for keeping them is totally forgotten? In a follow-up class discussion, relate those ideas to the force of tradition over the centuries.

2. Ask students to think about the following application of Reform Judaism's commitment to freedom of personal choice: Most Reform Jews don't keep kosher. They may feel that eating habits are not an effective way of expressing their religiosity, and object to the fact that kashrut intentionally keeps Jews from eating with non-Jews. But some Reform Jews choose not to eat shellfish or pork products. They may create a liberal kind of kashrut because they want a modern way to carry on an old, precious Jewish tradition. Other Reform Jews observe traditional kashrut in their homes because they want their parents and traditional members of the Jewish community to be able to eat at their table. A small minority keeps kosher all the time because they feel that it is an important way of expressing their belief and identifying with the Jewish people. All these opinions and practices—as well as many others—are found in the Reform Jewish community. Have students discuss these options with their parents and ask them the reasons they have chosen not to/to keep kosher. Then ask: What will you do when you have your own kitchen?

9
Organizations of Reform Judaism

FOCUS ON THE CHAPTER

This chapter talks about the three major institutions of Reform Judaism that were created and nurtured by Isaac Mayer Wise. These remain the foundation of the movement, and the paradigm for the organizational structure adopted by the other movements in Judaism. Although the Union of American Hebrew Congregations (UAHC) was created prior to Hebrew Union College-Jewish Institute of Religion (HUC-JIR) and the Central Conference of American Rabbis (CCAR), the role of the rabbinical school and the functions and services of the rabbinate are mentioned first because they are the touchstone for Jewish continuity. HUC-JIR, which in 1950 united the two separate schools—HUC, founded in 1875, and JIR, established in 1922—is the academic arm of the Reform movement. As such, it trains cantors, educators, communal service workers and rabbis and, in addition, offers advanced degrees in Judaica. The CCAR, the professional organization for rabbis, serves as a model for other professional groups in the Reform movement, such as NATE (the National Association of Temple Educators), NATA (the National Association of Temple Administrators) and the ACC (American Conference of Cantors). The UAHC, the lay organization of the Reform movement (made up of over 800 congregations in North America), serves the entire movement with a myriad of programs and services. All of these organizations, it should be noted, began as attempts to serve the *entire* American Jewish community (which, in the 1800s, liked to think of itself as "Hebrew"), rather than the special constituency that became known as the Reform movement. The chapter also mentions some of the more recent organizations of the movement and the specialized subsidiaries of the UAHC that serve the brotherhoods, sisterhoods and youth groups of Reform congregations.

APPROACHES

Introduce the study of this chapter by drawing a large triangle on the blackboard. Label one point UAHC, a second HUC-JIR, and the third CCAR. Read through the sections in Chapter Nine that explain the history and development of these three major bodies of the Reform movement in America. Review the story of the three organizations and their relationship to one another. You can end the class study of this chapter by asking students to consider the complementary—and sometimes conflicting—roles of freedom and union in relation to the Reform Jewish community. To aid their discussion, have students re-read pages 75–76 and page 82. Do the advantages of belonging to the UAHC outweigh the disadvantages? What about the times when the representatives of the movement speak in the name of every congregation and voice opinions that go counter to the position of your congregation? Is it worth paying dues to be part of an organization that represents Reform Judaism within the Jewish community and to the world at large? Conclude the discussion by having students vote on whether or not the congregation should remain in the Union or secede from it.

QUESTIONS FOR DISCUSSION

1. Discuss the purpose organizations serve in a religious movement. Show how the organizations of Reform Judaism which were established by Rabbi Isaac M. Wise, or emanated from the organizations he created, have been used as a paradigm for the rest of American Judaism. The other movements have adopted, for the most part, a similar organizational structure to that of the Reform movement.

2. Ask the class to imagine that it is 1850. They have just arrived in America and want to build a liberal Jewish movement that will work in their new country. What organizations would they need to have, and why? Compare their answers to the organizational structure of the Reform movement in its earliest years and to the Reform movement today.

3. After discussing all of the organizations in Chapter Nine that make up the Reform movement, encourage the class to try to determine if there is one single organization that leads/speaks for the Reform movement. What makes the UAHC the logical choice? One reason is its publishing activities. Most likely, many of your religious school textbooks have been published by the Union. So, too, the holiday books for young children. How does the creation of a textbook, or the writing of a curriculum, serve as a method of speaking for an entire movement? Discuss the force of education on the shaping of thought and choice.

4. Explore the connections your students and the congregation have with the various organizations in the Reform movement that are named in Chapter Nine, such as NFTS, NFTB, NFTY and the Union camps. Sample questions to consider: Are you using UAHC textbooks in your religious school? Does the congregation use the *Union Prayer Book* or *Gates of Prayer* (or other CCAR prayer books and publications) or some other prayer book altogether? Does the youth group belong to NFTY? Are youngsters encouraged to attend UAHC summer camps? Discussion should demonstrate that the congregation is intimately interwoven with the fabric of the movement.

CLASSROOM ENRICHMENT

1. The CCAR does many things to help the rabbis who belong to it. At each year's CCAR convention, your rabbi might study about Hasidism with a professor from one of the campuses of HUC-JIR; or listen to a psychiatrist talk about helping people face personal problems; or ask one of the CCAR committees for advice on questions ranging from whether a non-Jewish woman may bless the candles on Shabbat to the position Reform rabbis might take on abortion. The Responsa Committee studies traditional Jewish scholarly works to see what the great Jewish thinkers of the past have done in similar or comparable situations. The Bio-Medical Ethics Committee, to cite another example, consults with doctors and scientists in order to provide information for rabbis who have to help people facing difficult medical decisions. The Committee on Justice and Peace keeps an eye on ethical issues such as civil rights, or world hunger, or apartheid, and recommends to CCAR members ways for congregations to respond to each situation. Hold a mini-CCAR session in class. Divide the class into the committees mentioned above. Then have the class as a whole submit questions to each of the committees. The committees should then go into executive session to resolve the questions (where resolution is possible). As a follow-up to this activity, invite your rabbi to class to discuss the other ways in which he/she interacts with the CCAR and is served by it.

2. Review with the class the various logos of the Reform movement's institutions on page 80 in the text, and ask them to create an appropriate logo for the Reform movement as a whole.

3. Invite a member of the congregation who has attended a recent UAHC biennial to share his/her impressions of the gathering and some of the issues raised. Ask your guest to devote some time to the purpose and impact of the resolutions passed by the convention and to share a sense of the passion and variety of concerns of the delegates.

4. With the help of the class, create a broad outline of the subjects they would want/expect their rabbi, cantor and educator to have studied when they were training for their jobs (either at HUC-JIR or at another institution of higher Jewish learning). List the items suggested by the students on the blackboard. Now, compare it to the actual course of studies by inviting the rabbi, cantor and/or educator to come and discuss his/her training and education.

5. The new Reform prayer books, *Gates of Prayer, Gates of Repentance* and *Gates of the House,* address some themes that were not part of traditional liturgy or of the early Reform prayer books. These themes reflect events of modern history such as the Holocaust, the threat of nuclear warfare, the existence of the State of Israel, and other contemporary issues that engage our hopes and fears. If your class were writing a prayer book, what themes that represent the concerns of their generation would they want included? For help in getting started, look at the Table of Contents in *Gates of Prayer,* and especially at the section entitled "Special Themes."

BIOGRAPHY NOTEBOOK

Because this chapter is institutionally oriented, some of the people who played pivotal roles in the development of the Reform movement should have their biographical entries included here.

The UAHC is made up of over 800 Reform congregations in North America. Its international counterpart, the World Union for Progressive Judaism, is composed of the *national* organizations of the liberal movement around the world rather than individual congregations. **Israel Mattuck** was among the people responsible for creating the World Union. His biography should be included in the students' biography notebook while they are studying this chapter on the organizations of Reform Judaism.

Nelson Glueck, the well-known biblical archaeologist, was the president of HUC who oversaw its merger with JIR. Later, under his direction, the newly merged College-Institute expanded to include campuses in Los Angeles and in Jerusalem. Add Nelson Glueck to the biography notebook.

THINGS TO DO AT HOME

1. Ask students to make a scrapbook about Reform Judaism by collecting articles about all of the organizations in the Reform movement today. Use the magazine *Reform Judaism* for starters.

2. Have the class discuss with their parents their ideas of the ideal qualities for the perfect rabbi, cantor and educator.

3. Assign a student to write to the nearest campus of HUC-JIR and find out what you can about its program. Your temple office should have all of the addresses. If not, write to the National Office of Public Information, HUC-JIR, 1 West 4th Street, New York, NY 10012. When the information is received, have the student report his/her findings to the class.

Part 3
What Do Reform Jews Believe?

FOCUS

This section of the book deals with the beliefs that are basic to Reform Judaism and to all believing Jews—God, Torah and Israel (the Jewish people). The text explores the special Reform Jewish ways of understanding and interpreting each of these three central concerns.

To begin the study of Part Three, have your students "sound off" the words *God, Torah* and *Israel* (as if they were counting *one, two, three* in order to be divided into groups). The count should be done clearly and quickly. The repetition is designed to emphasize the saying of the Rabbis, quoted in the text's introduction to this section: "Israel, Torah, and the Holy One, blessed be He, are One."

CONTEST #3

Have students provide a photograph of themselves and/or members of their family "creating Torah for our time." Pages 93 and 107 of *Explaining Reform Judaism* should serve as examples. Hand-drawn entries may also be acceptable. Entries should be accompanied by an explanatory caption.

10
About God

FOCUS ON THE CHAPTER

This chapter will help you explain to your students the Reform Jewish understanding of God and God's relationship to the Jewish people and to every human being. It begins with a consideration of the traditional attempts to approach God, the personalization of God by attributing to God human characteristics and feelings—anthropomorphism and anthropopathism. As people's sense of historical experience and technical sophistication have grown over the centuries, the symbols for God and explanations of God have changed as well. The text next broaches the most difficult challenge to Jewish faith: the problem of evil. How can our tradition boast of a good and powerful God if all around us we see evil go unpunished?

The chapter concludes with a brief discussion about life after death. Jewish tradition accepts the idea that there is some kind of "life" after death, but offers little information apart from vague notions regarding bodily resurrection and the reunion of body and soul at the "end of days." Ultimately, Reform Judaism leaves these questions for each individual Jew to answer.

APPROACHES

Before you begin your study of Chapter Ten, you may want to set some ground rules for class discussion. Young people (and many adults, too) tend to be embarrassed when talking about their feelings about God. "God talk" is not a comfortable topic in our day, and is perceived by many people as something intensely personal. Many people, in fact, are uncomfortable admitting to a belief in God—let alone discussing it in a group situation. As a first premise, therefore, you must be certain that other students will not respond by laughing, ridiculing or challenging anyone willing to speak about God in class. Second, you must make clear to the class that *all* feelings must be considered valid and appropriate—even negative ones, so long as they are an honest expression of the feelings of that person. The environment for discussion must be open and supportive. Third, everyone who wishes to share feelings about God should be given the opportunity to do so. These ground rules should provide you with a good beginning for an in-depth search of personal feelings about God and the presence of God in the lives of individual Reform Jews. There will be an instant sense in the class that *this* discussion is somehow different, more intense and special than other topics; it may help students open up.

Because the whole God-idea is abstract and demands a sophisticated level of conceptualization, it may be helpful for your students to outline the chapter as you discuss it together. We would recommend that you work through this chapter paragraph by paragraph, unfolding each concept as it appears. Pay special attention to the lyric poetry that appears throughout the chapter. It is drawn from the prayer book (page 88), the Torah (page 87) and Holocaust literature (page 88). These poems should be extremely useful to you in communicating the concepts relating to human understanding of God. The photographs and the diagram can also help. Sometimes visual images convey much more than words. To conclude the study of this chapter, read aloud the concluding two paragraphs on page 89. Hopefully they will motivate your students to search actively for meaning and understanding throughout their lives, to be supportive of other people's efforts and to be open to the presence of God.

QUESTIONS FOR DISCUSSION

1. People's ideas about God have changed. Does this mean that God has changed? Long ago, people said that the sun was a living and powerful god. Later, others believed that the earth was flat and that the sun was a large star. They thought that the sun rose on one side of the earth, set on the other, and made the journey underneath during the night in order to be ready to come up again each morning. Centuries later, everyone "knew" that the earth was the center around which the sun revolved. Today, everyone is certain that the earth is one planet in our solar system and that all the spheres are in constant motion. Who knows what scientists will discover tomorrow? Had the positions of the earth and the sun changed during that time? Obviously not. What changed was people's understanding of that relationship. People change, relationships change, human needs are different at different times. It shouldn't surprise us, therefore, to see that some of the ways we have of talking and thinking about God are not the same as the ones people used before.

   Consider discussing with your students a personal application of the concept that constants can vary. For a specific example, use the shifting relationships of people to one another—each of us is a complete individual, yet we are also "different people" from the perspective of each of our various relationships (i.e., the same person can be daughter, sister, wife, mother, friend, boss, employee, adversary, etc.). Once the class is comfortable with this idea, ask them if the same sense of shifting relationships can be applied to God.

2. Toward the end of Chapter Ten, the authors address themselves to the problem of evil. Elicit from the class a definition of evil. Is evil always absolute? Always relative? Do varying perceptions of evil change their "evilness" or are some things bad for all people? Do your students think, for instance, that it is evil for cannibals to eat humans? *They* don't see anything wrong in that, and are only following the dictates of their society. What about Hitler? If he sincerely believed that what he was doing was correct, does that mitigate the evil? Examine the responsive reading on pages 249–250 of *Gates of Prayer* with the class, to expand your discussion. Ask the class to consider if evil is the absence of good or the opposite of good. Do they think that good can exist without a foundation in God?

3. Give the class examples of the variety of Jewish ideas about God, as presented in the text. Make a comparison chart on the board. Ask students which idea most clearly represents their own theological position. Is it strange that there are so many concepts of God when the *shema* says so clearly that "God is One"?

CLASSROOM ENRICHMENT

1. Look at two Friday evening services in *Gates of Prayer*—Service #VI and Service #VII. The first, in which God is never mentioned, is an attempt to present the viewpoint of "Jewish humanism" that is, a Judaism without God. How do your students react to the concept—and to the service itself? The second service, Service #VII, is intensely involved with God and the ways in which we can perceive God in the world. Do your students agree with the examples of God's "presence" in this service? Now, together with your students, examine two or three of the other Shabbat evening services in *Gates of Prayer*. Try to determine the editor's "God concept" in each service. Then compare these concepts to one another. (See Chaim Stern's characterizations of each service, in *Gates of Understanding*, edited by Lawrence Hoffman [New York: Central Conference of American Rabbis, 1977] for his statements about the focus of each service.)

2. Take the class on a tour of the synagogue and look for the symbols that represent God's presence. Then, go outdoors with the class and identify other, natural signs of God's presence. Ask the class to give examples of how one can identify God's presence in the world. Do some of the examples suggest that God is "limited in power—finite rather than infinite"? That is one of the concepts of God which the authors present, on page 88 of the textbook. How do your students react to this idea about God?

3. Chapter Ten is devoted entirely to people's attempts across the ages to apprehend God. God is given many names and described in many different ways in the Bible and in the prayer book. God is called "the Rock." Does this mean that God is a diamond, or a pillar of granite? Obviously not. The Bible says that God is a "rock of strength and a refuge," "an everlasting Rock," "my Rock and my Redeemer." To what qualities that people associate with God is the Bible referring? (You might want to show the class some photographs of the rocky mountains in Sinai and in the Negev. They are imposing and majestic and can help students understand why our ancestors chose "Rock" as an image for God.) We have continued to use this symbol in modern times; it still resonates for us; but it is probably not one our generation would have selected. The same is true of names for God like "king," "lord," "master of the universe" or even "my shepherd." We are comfortable with these descriptions because we are familiar with them, but they are not part of everyday life for us as they were for the people who wrote the prayers.

   List as many traditional names and symbolic identifications for God as the students can come up with. Give students copies of *Gates of Prayer* and have them find the *amidah* (*Tefilah*). Together, examine the first two blessings (the *avot* and the *gevurot*). How many of the names and descriptions of God listed there can they identify? Does that mean that Jews worship many different Gods? What images might we use today to describe God as powerful? As loving protector? Have your students try creating a "modern" name or image for God. Make a list of God-words either from Jewish tradition or from your students' own vocabulary.

BIOGRAPHY NOTEBOOK

   Rabbi Eugene Borowitz is not only the co-author of our text, *Explaining Reform Judaism*, but he is also one of the foremost Jewish theologians speaking frankly about God in America today. Have your students prepare an entry on Eugene Borowitz for the biography notebook.

Since Borowitz uses some of the same highly personalized God language as did **Martin Buber,** you may want to take this opportunity to have a biography entry prepared on Martin Buber as well.

THINGS TO DO AT HOME

1. On page 87, the text mentions various challenges to God from our tradition. Abraham, Moses and Jeremiah argued with God; Rabbi Levi Yitzhak from Berditchev told God that God was not acting fairly and that God's deeds needed to be judged according to God's laws (Torah). Ask your students to compose a meditation "challenging" God about all of the evil in the world and bring their meditations into class. Make copies either of all of their meditations or a selection of what the class has written and redistribute them to all the students. On which points do they agree?

2. Based on the concluding section of the chapter, make up a list of questions with the class and ask them to survey their family and their friends on the subject of life after death. Have the students bring the results of their surveys to the next session of the class for discussion.

11
About the Jewish People

FOCUS ON THE CHAPTER

This chapter, more than any other, speaks abut each and every Jew, regardless of political or religious ideology. It is "About the Jewish People"—a very diverse group, as is clearly illustrated in the photomontage on page 90. Is Judaism a religion, a nation or an ethnic group? Chapter Eleven examines this question, one that has been debated by Jews and non-Jews alike for centuries. The text first considers the problems inherent in each definition. For instance, is an American Jew who accepts the "nation" definition of the Jewish people disloyal to the United States? The chapter then determines that we are a religious *people,* a concept that also involves national aspects. The various ways in which one becomes a Jew— by birth or by conversion—underscore this conclusion. In fact the problem with "normal" attempts to define Judaism lies not so much with the unusual nature of Judaism as with its affinity to non-Christian rather than to Christian religions—particularly since the word *religion* itself really fully applies only to Christianity, and there is no English word that accurately describes Judaism.

APPROACHES

In order for your students to thoroughly understand this chapter, divide the class into three groups—*religion, nation, people.* Ask them to arrange their chairs so that each group is seated in its own circle. All of the students in each group must then read the section of the textbook appropriate to their topic and to discuss, as a group, the validity of that definition and the problems inherent in it. Let them know that they must argue in favor of the "correctness" of their definition, whatever their personal reservations. This means that they must find ways to defend Judaism as a religion, Judaism as a nation, and Judaism as a people against possible criticisms from students in the other groups. After they have finished the reading, talked through their opinions and reached some sort of consensus, have them turn their chairs so that each group faces the other two, forming a triangle. Now give each group the opportunity to convince the others that *their* definition of Judaism is the correct one. Unless the students themselves draw the logical conclusion, it will be your responsibility to determine when to end the debate and resolve the conflict by suggesting that all of the definitions are correct but that none tells the whole story. Use the example of how one becomes a Jew (pages 98–99) as proof, and conclude with the concept introduced in the final section of the chapter (on page 99), that our "mix of faith and people" is not as unusual as we sometimes think.

QUESTIONS FOR DISCUSSION

1. Using the leading question that introduces Chapter Eleven, "What Makes a Person Jewish?", analyze with the class the complex variety of factors that are part of Judaism. Write the list on the board and then determine which are essential elements. Discuss Bernhard Felsenthal's definition with the class (you will find it in the biography section of this *Guide*).

2. A question regarding the centuries-long love of Jews in the Diaspora for Israel: How can you want to "return" to a place you've never been?

3. Does the existence of an independent Israel create a problem of dual loyalty for American Jews? In recent years anti-Semitic charges have been leveled, especially during the Jonathan Pollard spy scandal. At that time Vice President George Bush called on Jews *to continue* their support for Israel: "Citizen advocacy strengthens our country. It gives America vitality. It's the reason why America is so great." What did he mean? Do your students agree with him? How do they feel about charges of dual loyalty? And another question: Should American Jews be able to have dual citizenship in Israel and the United States if they desire it?

4. What changes took place in the relationship of Reform Judaism to Zionism between the Pittsburgh Platform of 1885 and the 1930s? Discuss why, in the light of the events that were soon to take place (in the late 1930s and 1940s), this change is such a significant and important one.

5. Beginning on page 97 in the textbook is a discussion about the make-up of the American population. Review the difference between "melting pot" and "mosaic" (or "orchestra" or "salad"). Discuss the philosophic thrust of each term and draw with your students the logical consequences of each one for Jewish peoplehood (ethnicity) in America.

CLASSROOM ENRICHMENT

1. Spend a little time on the Zionist activities and leadership roles of Rabbis Stephen S. Wise and Abba Hillel Silver. Many of Silver's speeches have been recorded. You might want to play one for your class.

2. As the summary to this chapter indicates, the religious model for Judaism is a difficult one for people to understand easily because our terminology in English has been shaped by the influence of Christianity on the Western world. Since Judaism is more than a religion, a nation and a people, can the class come up with a good word to describe what Judaism *is*? Use a dictionary for help, but don't be surprised if your combined efforts fail to produce a satisfactory single word definition. Conclude by having your students, either in discussion form or as a written exercise, complete these sentences: Judaism is a religion because . . . . Judaism is more than just a religion because. . . .

BIOGRAPHY NOTEBOOK

Assign a student to prepare a capsule biography on **Rabbi Bernhard Felsenthal,** whose definition of Jewishness is appropriate to this chapter. Now is also a good time to assign **Rabbi Judah Magnes**, a Reform leader of the American Zionist movement.

THINGS TO DO AT HOME

1. As a research project, in order to emphasize the diversity of the Jewish people, assign a couple of students to try and find out how many Jewish languages there are. Ask them each to prepare a brief presentation so that they can tell the class a little about each one.

2. Ask students to discuss with their parents the country/countries from which their families came to America. What language(s) did they speak? Are there any photographs or documents relating to the family history? Are there any special foods the family eats or traditions they practice that come from traditions based on the background of the student's family? How many of these belong to the "religion" part of being Jewish? The "nation" part? The "people" part? Devote a few minutes of class time at the session following this assignment to student "show and tell" about their family backgrounds.

3. The section called "Nation Problems in America" reviews the reversal of the Reform movement's official position on Israel since the time of the Pittsburgh Platform. Today the Reform Jewish presence in Israel is a pronounced one. Assign a student to prepare a presentation for the class about the first Reform kibbutz, Yahel, Kibbutz Lotan and the Garin Arava.

12

About the Torah, the Bible and Jewish Tradition

FOCUS ON THE CHAPTER

Chapter Twelve looks at Torah from the perspective of Reform Judaism. Reform Judaism maintains that God did not write the Bible, but that it is instead the work of inspired human beings. As the text explains, when the *Tanakh* (the Hebrew acronym for Bible) says "Thus says the Lord," we should understand this to mean "a religious genius sensed what God wanted." The idea that God is the inspiration for Torah helps Reform Judaism maintain the sanctity and centrality of the text.

Although our ancestors may have been religious geniuses, they were not perfect. They could not anticipate the needs of our day. Thus, each generation has a responsibility to "add to Torah"—with Torah understood in its broadest sense—in its own special way. This dynamic view of Torah is indispensable to Reform Judaism. We remain the people of Israel, trying to serve God today by making "living Torah" as best we can. Chapter Twelve concludes with another discussion of the place of God, this time in reference to Torah. The one God about whom our ancestors wrote is the same one God we experience—we simply have new and different ways of thinking about God. These new ways come from what we have learned from science, human behavior, philosophy and personal experience.

APPROACHES

Although your students come from liberal Jewish families, they may not have previously confronted the questions about the nature and authorship of Torah which this chapter asks. As a result, you may want to invite parents to come to class and join in the discussion on this subject. You will want to alert your students to the fact that this chapter may challenge what they were previously taught or had assumed. The question of the authorship of the Bible is still a sensitive subject for many people.

Since many young people are familiar with and intrigued by the *Guinness Book of World Records*, the data contained in the introductory paragraph of Chapter Twelve (on page 100) can be a springboard for the rest of your discussion. Give each student (and any parent who has joined you for this session) a sheet of paper with the question "Who wrote the Bible?" at the top of each side of the paper. One side should be labeled 1 and the other 2. Ask everyone to write an answer to the question on side 1 without turning over the page, looking at the textbook or discussing the question with anyone else. After they have finished, ask them to open the book and read the section of Chapter Twelve that asks the same question (parents can share books with their children). Now, have them turn to side 2 and answer the question on the basis of what they have learned. When they have finished, have them circle any discrepancies they see. Discuss these together.

The discussion should continue: If our ancestors wrote the Torah and God did not write the Torah, can we too write Torah? The answer is yes, and pages 105–108 provide some guidance as to how "writing Torah" is possible today. Using a large flip chart, write down the kinds of things students (and parents) believe will continue the growth of Torah today (pages 106–108 give some suggestions). The discussion should now return to its starting point: Traditional Jews believe that God is the author of the Torah. If we reject that notion, where do we find God in Torah and why do we still consider the Torah sacred? Some of the new ways for thinking about God are included in the closing pages of the chapter.

QUESTIONS FOR DISCUSSION

1. Mohammed, the prophet of Islam, called the Jews "People of the Book." Although he probably meant *the* book, that is, the Bible, our people has understood the phrase more broadly. What have been the most important Jewish books across the ages? How have Jews studied biblical texts over the years? Why do liberal Jews study these same texts today, if we don't believe that the Torah was literally given by God? The section called "An Imperfect Creation" should help in this area.

2. Revelation is the term used to describe when God "appears" either directly or indirectly to human beings. According to Jewish tradition, revelation occurred on Mount Sinai; Reform Jews believe that revelation is an ongoing, evolving process. Discuss the difference in these two concepts with your class.

3. Teach the students a little about the "documentary" approach to the study of Bible. Basically, this approach analyzes the text as a literary/historical document and sees four "strands"—E, in which God is referred to primarily as *elohim*; J, in which God is called *Y-H-V-H*; D, for the author of Deuteronomy; and P, for the Priests who made additions in various places and may have served as the redactors of the entire document. The presumption of multiple authorship, obviously, contradicts the idea that the entirety of sacred scripture was "dictated" by God to Moses, and the presence of priestly "editors" adds *their* interests and authority as a further coloration of the text. Perhaps it is their doing that there is so much emphasis upon the centrality of the Temple and the sacrificial system in the Torah.

   Raise with the class the possibility that taking a scholarly, critical approach to this subject diminishes the integrity and centrality of Torah. Try to help them understand that it is not necessary to suspend faith in order to deal with the specifics of this greatest of all books, that the brilliance of the people who wrote and edited the Bible is, if anything, enhanced by our realization that they were sensitive to the needs of their times and understood how to achieve the goals, they trusted, were inspired by God.

4. Once we accept the idea that people wrote the Bible, we aren't surprised to discover Bible stories similar to those of other groups in the ancient Near East. Relate this example to your students: There is a Babylonian myth about a flood that would have destroyed the world except that one man built an ark, stocked it with animals and rode out the storm. What astonishes us, however, are not the similarities but the important differences between the Babylonian account and the biblical one. In the Bible story, God wanted to destroy the world because people had become violent and treated each other wickedly. In the Babylonian account, the gods got bored with the noise human beings made and decided to get rid of the annoyance. Noah was saved because he was righteous.

Utnapishtim, the Babylonian hero, was saved because he was friendly with one of the gods. The other gods were furious when they found out that Utnapishtim had survived the flood—until they got hungry for sacrifices. When Utnapishtim offered a sacrifice in thanks for being saved, the gods "crowded around it like flies." How very different is the end of the flood story in the Bible! God responds to Noah's thanksgiving sacrifice by making a covenant with him and his descendants. God promises to bring no more floods, and Noah is commanded in return to live in decency and to rule the earth but not be cruel to animals or murder people. Unlike its parallels in Near Eastern literature, the Bible teaches an amazingly high standard of good and evil. It sees possibilities for human progress far beyond anything we find among the ancient Hebrews' neighbors. Why did the biblical authors adapt common myths of human origins and prehistoric catastrophes to suit their own situations and belief in God rather than creating their own stories? (If you want to look at some of the original sources with which the Bible stories may be compared, see James Pritchard, *Ancient Near Eastern Texts Relating to the Old Testament*.)

5. The authors say that in every generation people have the ability to add to Torah. This idea becomes possible once we accept that the Torah does not have divine authorship. Using pages 105–108 as a basis for ideas, ask students to suggest some specific ways in which Jews have added to Torah in this generation. You might want to confront them with this question: Are non-religious Jews (or non-Jews, for that matter) who make important scientific discoveries creating Torah in our day? Based on what they have already learned in *Explaining Reform Judaism,* which innovations of the Reform movement do your students think have not become part of Torah tradition because too many Reform Jews did not find them acceptable?

CLASSROOM ENRICHMENT

1. The textbook speaks of divine inspiration—"a religious genius sensed what God wanted"—rather than divine revelation. Have the class make a list of phrases in the Bible that may be translated as "a religious genius sensed what God wanted." Two obvious examples are "the word of God came to me" and "God said to Moses." There are many others.

2. Have the students reread the section "Who Wrote the Bible?" on page 101. As a class, find the biblical passages cited and read them aloud. What are the contradictions or differing versions in each case? How do these textual discrepancies reinforce the contention that the Bible is both an "imperfect creation" *and* "the greatest of all books"?

BIOGRAPHY NOTEBOOK

   Julian Morgenstern, who served as President of Hebrew Union College, was a world-renowned Bible scholar. Since this chapter focuses on the place of the Bible in Reform Judaism, it is appropriate that his biography be included in the Notebook during study of this chapter.

THINGS TO DO AT HOME

1. Ask students to make a Bible checklist at home. Have them begin by looking for complete

Bibles and individual biblical books. In preparation, review the names of the books of the Bible and the divisions of the *Tanakh* as well as the various possible names for the Torah (i.e., Pentateuch, Five Books of Moses). When they have completed that search, they should look for other books that may have been inspired by a biblical text (or work significant enough to be considered "Torah"), and then do the same with their family's collection of artwork, sculpture and music. Compare each family's collection of "living Torah."

2. For many early Reformers, *ethical monotheism* was an acceptable definition of Judaism. This means that, to them, ethical behavior—with God as the foundation for good—was the most important part of being Jewish. Is that idea still applicable? Why do most Reform Jews today feel that it is an inadequate definition? What that we have learned about human behavior does it omit? If one takes the notion of ethical monotheism to its most extreme conclusion one can arrive at a "religion" like Ethical Culture. Assign a student to present the historical background of the Society for Ethical Culture. Information can be found in the *Encyclopedia Judaica*. Compare the Society for Ethical Culture to Reform Judaism. Apart from the fact that Ethical Culture carries the idea of ethical monotheism to a ridiculous extreme, it also provides a "religion" totally devoid of ritual and ceremony. Initially, some students may find this idea appealing. To challenge them, explain the value of ceremonies to people's lives. Use examples such as birthday celebrations, parades on Thanksgiving, fireworks on the 4th of July, half-time bands at football games to make your point.

Part 4
What is a Reform Jew Supposed to Do?

FOCUS

Once Reform Judaism denied the binding authority of halakhah, the obligation to fulfill mitzvot and act responsibly shifted from a religious imperative to an individual option. This section of *Explaining Reform Judaism* focuses on how individual Reform Jews ought to behave. As you have done with the previous parts of the textbook, read the questions and comments in this introductory section aloud to your students. Assign each question to a group of students. It will be their responsibility to alert the class to the fact that "their" question is being answered when that topic comes up during class discussion.

CONTEST #4

Many parts of Section Four lend themselves to slogans. In fact, a number of pages in Chapter Fourteen are dedicated to *pit-ga-meem,* sayings and aphorisms that are a kind of sloganeering for Jewish concerns. The object of this contest is to provide an *existing* slogan (single line commercials, well known phrases associated with a cartoon character, a movie, book or song title, or any one line from a song, etc.) that captures the spirit, essence and message of any part of Section Four, with an appropriate parenthetical explanation. The first example we offer comes form Chapter Thirteen: "His master's voice" (the prophet Amos). The second relates to Chapter Fifteen and presents both sides of the picture: "Never on Sunday" from the movie of that title, and "Rats," from the "Peanuts" comic strip—both relating to the decision of the majority of the Reform movement to keep Shabbat on Saturday rather than continuing with the controversial innovation of a Sunday Sabbath.

13

The Reform Jewish Emphasis on Ethics

FOCUS ON THE CHAPTER

Throughout its history, Reform Judaism has de-emphasized the role of ritual and stressed ethical behavior in its place. This chapter explores the central role of ethics in Reform Judaism. The focus of the chapter is the paradigm for ethical behavior, the biblical prophet. The text has chosen Amos as the prophet *par excellence,* because his life of service exemplifies the ethical ideal for which Reform Judaism strives. He is the first literary prophet, that is, the first prophet to have a book which bears his name and records his prophecy. The textbook shows the clever way in which Amos functioned. He went north from Judah to prophesy against the abuses of the people of Israel, but he did not begin his criticism with the people of Israel. Instead, he directed his remarks against the other nations, the enemies of Israel, and then against the excesses of the Judeans, his own people. Only then, when his listeners were sympathetic to his message, did he direct his diatribe against Israel and tell them why they deserved God's anger. The early Reformers saw in prophets like Amos a way to shape their Jewish identity. Chapter Thirteen ends with a question that goes right to the heart of the matter: If the message of the prophets is universal, then why stay Jewish? What need is there for Judaism? The authors answer with a strong affirmation of Judaism and its passionate commitment to ethical *action,* a focus distinct from the primary emphasis on "faith" in other religions, particularly Christianity.

APPROACHES

Begin your study of this chapter by confronting your students with the questions posed at the beginning of Chapter Thirteen. These are very tough questions, and young people do face such situations in their day-to-day struggle with peer pressure. Direct the responses toward positive ways of dealing with unethical situations and peer pressure. Let the class attempt to role play the hypothetical case presented in the textbook and find ways of getting themselves out of unpleasant and potentially frightening experiences.

Then retell the story of Amos, reading selectively form pages 113–116 and including the quotations from the Bible contained in the text. Ask the class to imagine how they would feel after receiving Amos' message. Would they be motivated to repent? To change? Or would they rise up against Amos? Remind them that religion played a more central role in people's lives in earlier generations than it does in ours. How do the students think Amos felt when he had to deliver such a rough message from God? Look at the etching of Jeremiah on page 117. How does the artist depict him? Is he unhappy because of what he sees the Jewish people doing, or because he must be God's "prophet of doom," or perhaps both?

QUESTIONS FOR DISCUSSION

1. Much of Chapter Thirteen is devoted to Amos, the first "literary" prophet. The term, used but not explained in the text, simply means that a book of the Bible bears his name and contains his teachings. Non-literary prophets, like Elijah, are remembered more for their actions than for what they said, because their words were not so carefully recorded and their deeds make up part of the narrative of other books (like the Book of Kings). Amos gave the Israelites God's "warnings." Explain to the class that ancient people understood natural disasters and extraordinary or freak natural occurrences as "signs" from God that trouble was impending—or, depending upon their severity, as punishment in themselves.

   Amos told the Israelites that God was not really interested in their sacrifices. "Sacrifices" (i.e., offerings) can be interpreted—and reinterpreted—in many ways. Some, obviously, are noble and positive (parents who sacrifice their own pleasures or leisure time in order to do important things for their children; people who give contributions to worthy causes under emergency situations, etc.). But sacrifices as Temple offerings were often for the purpose of asking God to help bring about personal desires. What if we reinterpret the *negative* implications (the things the prophets were criticizing) as "bribes" or as "tainted money"? What if someone wished to make such a contribution to the synagogue, or to the Federation? Yet the founder of the Salvation Army willingly accepted money that came from unethical sources (gambling, prostitution, theft, "laundered" cash) and boasted that he would "wash it clean in the blood of the Lamb." What did he mean? Why is such an attitude unacceptable to Reform Judaism? (Hint: use the prophetic exhortation.)

2. Are there any prophets in the Reform movement (people who speak out and accuse Israel [the people and/or the land] of "evil")? What criteria for good do such prophets use? Look at Maurice Eisendrath (see the biography notebook section). Are their criticisms and reproaches useful? Successful? Harmful? Why?

3. The improvement of society, a focus of Reform Judaism and one of the subjects of this chapter, is not strictly a Jewish concern. Yet Jews have been disproportionately active in this work. Give the class relevant examples. Civil rights is an easy and interesting one to document—particularly since it is a mixed bag of exciting activity, great successes, heartache and tragedy, misunderstandings and a continuing need for dialogue and action. Ask the class if they think that Reform Judaism's emphasis will—or should—continue to be on ethical behavior now that there is a shift in the Reform movement toward greater traditional observance.

CLASSROOM ENRICHMENT

1. Set up several improvisations of unethical situations (shoplifting, lying, cheating on an exam). Ask your students for their reactions and an explanation of why these represent *unethical* (as well as *illegal*) behavior. Are some ethical actions illegal? Are certain legal provisions unethical? How do your students think such situations should be dealt with? What course of action would they take? Is civil disobedience justified for every situation? (Examples might include not only civil rights infringements in our country but also Jewish resistance during the Holocaust, "illegal" immigration to Palestine during the British Mandate (Aliyah Bet), the activities of the Marranos—and similar activities by the Jews in Russia today.) As a follow-up, appoint a student to serve as the prophetic voice of conscience for the class. Consider choosing one of the more vocal, popular students. This

should help assure maximum effectiveness and student cooperation. Let that student react to and/or evaluate class behavior.

2. Once divine authority is removed from Torah, mitzvot are no longer commandments; they have become optional. Some people have chosen to translate mitzvot as "demandments." Have students list the ethical "demandments" that God makes of them in their daily life, focusing specifically on ethical *behavior*. Ask them to comment on the difference between "commandments" and "demandments."

3. Either assign this as a written exercise or appoint a "scribe" and, together with the class, rewrite the story of Amos, on page 113 in the textbook, in a modern setting.

BIOGRAPHY NOTEBOOK

Rabbi Maurice Eisendrath, who died in 1972, was president of the Union of American Hebrew Congegations. Many people in your congregation may still remember him, particularly because of his passionate commitment to ethics in Reform Judaism. A number of UAHC activities, including a high school program in Israel, are named in his memory. Since the focus of Chapter Thirteen is on ethics, have an entry on Eisendrath presented for the Biography Notebook at this time.

Many of the radical Reformers, who sought to excise ritual from Reform Judaism, substituted ethics for ceremonial observance. **Rabbi Emil Hirsch** was one radical Reformer whose radicalism led him to place tremendous emphasis on the ethical aspects of Judaism. He was also a chief proponent of the Sunday Sabbath. Add Rabbi Hirsch to the Notebook.

THINGS TO DO AT HOME

1. Assign each student a biblical prophet to research at home. At the next session of class, ask the students to "be" their prophet and react to classroom happenings as they believe that prophet would have done.

2. Have students read and discuss the prophetic texts in Chapter Thirteen with members of their family. What is their reaction to Reform Judaism's emphasis on prophetic ethics? How would these family members describe themselves: as people who live by these ethics in a general way or as individuals who are (or were) actively involved in specific activities of ethical obligation?

14
Reform Jewish Duties: Ethics Plus

FOCUS ON THE CHAPTER

Reform Judaism today does not find ethics alone sufficient. Reform Jews have other obligations as well. The initial pages of Chapter Fourteen (pages 120–123) list and describe these obligations, which the Central Conference of American Rabbis has divided into nine broad categories. As the categories are general and a bit abstract, the text suggests, on page 124, ways in which individuals can meet the demands of these obligations. It also includes several pages of quotations from rabbinic literature and other models of Jewish thought, to amplify and make specific the range of duties of a Reform Jew.

Prepare to teach this chapter by distributing large sheets of paper to each group of two students whom you have paired together. Assign one of the nine categories of ethical obligation to each group. Ask them to read the definition for their category in Chapter Fourteen (pages 120–123) and to list the activities that fall into their category. They can use the suggestions on page 124 as starters. After they have finished, post the papers around the room. Give everyone time to look at each list carefully. Then, going list by list, see which activities students have been involved in during the year. Which have the most current student participation? Which have the least? Finally, assign each of the quotations listed on pages 125–129 to individual students. Ask them to think about the quote, determine its meaning and then, in their own words, share their insights with the class. Ask the class to indicate the kind of situation in which such a quotation might give them guidance. Use the questions on page 129 for help.

QUESTIONS FOR DISCUSSION

1. Chapter Fourteen is devoted primarily to exploring the obligations of individuals. To help broach that subject, ask the class to explain why the Talmud says that it is a parent's obligation to teach his child how to swim. Draw from your students an understanding that this seemingly isolated and perhaps irrelevant example is used to establish a broad category of obligation—that is, if a parent must do this, how much more so must the parent do other things. And if this is what a parent should do for his/her child, how much more so. . .

2. Specifics need to be added to each category of obligation listed in Chapter Fourteen. (For example: What does it mean for Reform Jews to keep Shabbat and the Holy Days?) See how well the class can do. How do we prepare properly for the choices we make as Reform Jews? Does the preparation end at bar/bat mitzvah or confirmation, etc. or should it be a continuous process throughout life? Why?

3. After you have discussed each one in detail, ask the class for suggestions to add to the list of specific obligations on page 124. Have one student act as scribe and write these suggestions on the board.

CLASSROOM ENRICHMENT

1. Assign a quotation (pages 125–129 in the text, or from the worksheet) to each student and give everyone an opportunity to interpret it to the class—through words, pictures, songs, or a combination of media. Help students figure out ways to implement the obligations, either implicit or explicit, contained in the quotation.

2. One of the ways a traditional Jew expresses his religious position and reminds himself of his Jewish obligations is to wear a kippah all the time. How might you, as a liberal Jew, express your pattern of observance and remind yourself of your Jewish obligations?

BIOGRAPHY NOTEBOOK

Among the Reform Jewish duties mentioned in this chapter is the obligation to help Jewish survival throughout the world. **Lillian Montagu,** an English social worker and magistrate, exemplified this commitment to Jewish continuity. Have a student prepare her biography for the Notebook.

THINGS TO DO AT HOME

1. Ask students to discuss the nine categories of Reform obligation with their parents. After they have determined specific ways to implement each, have them make a family pledge to fulfill each category in the way they have agreed upon.

2. Have students choose and write one or two of the quotations on pages 125–129 and, during Shabbat dinner, talk with their parents about the significance and implications of the passages. Students should be prepared to summarize the discussion, either orally or in writing.

15

How We Decide Just What We Need to Do

FOCUS ON THE CHAPTER

This chapter is concerned with the way Reform Judaism makes decisions about specific issues or practices. To illustrate the process, the textbook presents three important test cases. Case One describes the "equality of women," a concern that continues to pervade all aspects of Reform Judaism. The second case is the attempt by early, radical Reformers to create a viable option to the poorly attended Saturday morning service. Although their experiment failed, a parallel attempt to respond to the same problem led to the establishment of a late Friday evening service, a successful change. Rabbis and lay people have different reactions to Case Three: the question of whether or not rabbis should officiate at intermarriages is a delicate one with no simple answers.

APPROACHES

These cases illustrate well the kind of changes that continue to challenge Reform Judaism. Either assign students to read about each case before it is discussed in detail, or begin the session by reading, or summarizing, the relevant section of the textbook. The following questions should serve as guidelines for dealing with each of the cases.

1. What is the essential problem that the Reform movement is addressing here?

2. Has traditional Judaism attempted to deal with this problem in the past?

3. Did the Reform movement make earlier attempts to resolve the problem? Explain.

4. How was the change decided upon?

5. How was it implemented?

6. Was the change successful? Did it solve the problem? Was an alternative solution more satisfactory? If so, why?

7. Does the solution still seem to be working? Has the problem resurfaced in a different form? And if so, what should be done about it today?

QUESTIONS FOR DISCUSSION

1. Case One, beginning on page 131, speaks of the stress on equality in Reform Judaism, especially for women. Why has Reform Judaism parted with traditional Judaism's concept of woman's role as childbearer and housekeeper? Women can now be rabbis and cantors, read from the Torah, wear tallit and kippah and put on tefillin (if they choose to do so). How comfortable are your students with having women wear ritual garments (like kippot and tallitot) traditionally assigned to men? Do any women in your congregation wear ritual garments? Would your female students? What about when the woman is a rabbi or cantor? Ask your students to consider to corollary: having made women equal to men, how do we now make men equal to women? Would it be acceptable for a man to light the Shabbat candles, for instance? Does patrilineal descent bring equality to men in Jewish religious life? What about new parenting roles for fathers? Invite a woman rabbi or cantor to class to share her experiences with your students.

   Do obstacles to full male/female equality still exist in your synagogue? If there are any, have the class choose one and figure out how to overcome it.

2. As part of this sense of equality, Chapter Fifteen notes, men and women were no longer seated separately in the synagogue. Thus, the mood of the worship service changed. A sense of family devotion became part of the experience of attending services. It even gave birth to a lovely custom that speaks of family harmony and the spirit of Shabbat. This custom could not exist until families began coming to services together—and sitting together. Now, when the service was over and people would say *shabbat shalom,* parents and children—no longer sitting apart from one another—began to turn and greet each other with a Shabbat kiss. This custom beautifully expresses many of the "obligations" caring Jews feel and demonstrates how Reform innovations can give greater meaning to traditional ideas. How do the students react to this custom? Can a case be made for the idea that when men and women (or boys and girls) sit together at services, they distract one another from prayer?

3. Case Two is concerned with a radical solution to poor attendance at Shabbat services. Have contemporary Jews created any new alternatives to the Sunday Sabbath in response to the renewed challenges of poor Friday night and Saturday morning attendance? Why, in some congregations, do large numbers of people no longer attend Friday night services as regularly as they once did? Now that so many people no longer work on weekends, should the Reform movement consider once again making the Shabbat morning service the primary one of the week? Have the class devise a plan to increase attendance at worship services.

CLASSROOM ENRICHMENT

1. On page 130, the text speaks of decisions that many congregations have had to make during the last ten years. Every congregational choice, whether it relates to purchasing a new prayer book, or replacing members of the staff, or redecorating the sanctuary or social hall, or taking a stand on social action issues, will most likely dissatisfy some of its members. What options does that leave the individual congregant in his/her right to choose? Invite to your classroom someone who served as a member of the temple's ritual committee while discussions about whether or not to adopt *Gates of Prayer* and *Gates of*

Repentance took place. Let him/her tell the class what happened, including the pros and cons of the argument.

2. As Case Three states, the matter of rabbis officiating at intermarriages is a difficult and delicate one. What is the difference in philosophy between a rabbi who officiates at a mixed marriage and one who co-officiates with non-Jewish clergy at a similar ceremony (and perhaps even at one which takes place in a church)? Should congregational restrictions be placed on the members of intermarried families? For example, should a non-Jewish spouse be permitted to hold office on the synagogue's Board? Or be allowed to vote at congregational meetings? Or serve on congregational committees? Should intermarriages be announced in the local Jewish community newspaper? Congratulations given in the synagogue bulletin? Why? Why not? Have students debate the issue of rabbinic officiation at mixed marriages. Invite your rabbi to explain his/her position on intermarriage to your class.

BIOGRAPHY NOTEBOOK

A number of men played key roles in helping the Reform movement in America develop, grow and change to meet changing needs. **Kaufmann Kohler** was unhappy about the poor number of worshipers attending services on Saturday, so he instituted a Sunday service while he was the rabbi of the Sinai Congregation in Chicago. The Sunday service did not become successful there, however, until Emil Hirsch succeeded him as rabbi. When Kohler took a pulpit in New York and failed again at attempting to institute Sunday services, he changed his position and became adamantly opposed to Sunday services. Since part of this chapter focuses on the Sunday Sabbath, a student should be asked to prepare biographical material on Rabbi Kohler.

Jacob Z. Lauterbach was an important member of the CCAR Responsa Committee, and served as its chairperson for many years. During his tenure, he issued an influential responsum permitting the use of birth control. At the same time, he issued a responsum opposing the ordination of women. Since this chapter focuses on how to decide what to do, and because one of the three cases, in particular, reflects decisions reached by Lauterbach, it would be a good time to enter his biography.

THINGS TO DO AT HOME

1. At home with family members, discuss the challenge of intermarriage. Why do they feel the way they do? Were you surprised by their attitudes?

16
Our Relation to the State of Israel

FOCUS ON THE CHAPTER

When Reform Judaism was in its infancy, the Emancipation represented new and exciting possibilities for Jews who wished to modernize. The idea of citizenship, of *belonging,* was incredibly attractive. The land of Israel, by contrast, represented the painful memory of the destruction of the Temple and the dispersion of Jews throughout the world. And so, the longing for Zion was dismissed as unrealistic by Reformers who wished to avail themselves of the opportunities of the Emancipation and the freedom of life in America. Since those early years, Reform Judaism has come full circle. The Reform movement is now a firm, unyielding supporter of the State of Israel. Chapter Sixteen focuses on the quest of the Reform movement to make a home for itself in Israel and to make a central place for Israel in the hearts of Reform Jews. The photographs in this chapter tell the story quite effectively.

APPROACHES

Begin your study of Chapter Sixteen by finding out how many of your students have been to Israel. If you have been there recently, or the rabbi, or any of the students' parents, you might want to share slides of the places mentioned in the chapter with the class. It would be excellent if the institutions of Reform Judaism such as Kibbutz Yahel in the Negev and the Jerusalem campus of HUC-JIR could be included among the slides shown. As pages 140 to the middle of page 145 provide background for the rest of the chapter, you may want to summarize that material for your students or prepare a list of questions requiring the students to review those pages in the textbook in order to find the answers. Finally, ask your students for their ideas about our responsibilities to the State of Israel. Suggest that they consult pages 149–150 in the textbook for suggestions.

QUESTIONS FOR DISCUSSION

1. Chapter Sixteen speaks of the existence of the State of Israel as a given fact. Is it possible for your students to imagine a world without Israel, which came into existence many years before they were born? Would they feel more or less secure as Jews? Would their lives be any different? How?

2. Discuss the change in the Reform movement's relationship with Israel, particularly noted on pages 145–148. To what extent was the change the result of the Columbus Platform of 1936? How much was it a response to the Holocaust combined with a surge of Jewish pride at the establishment of the State of Israel in 1948? Or was the change, rather, a

response to world anti-Jewish sentiments felt throughout the country by Reform as well as traditional Jews?

3. The anti-Israel propaganda which often comes into our community is not always intended only as an attack on Israel. All too frequently, anti-Israelism masks an effort to defame all Jews ("Zionism is racism," in fact, is nothing more than new clothing for the old anti-Semitism.) How well-informed are your students? Can they answer criticism and challenges by their non-Jewish friends and secular school classmates? As part of your consideration of the closing paragraphs of Chapter Sixteen, raise these issues with your students.

4. Chapter Sixteen deals with a difficult problem regarding pluralism and the State of Israel. Non-Orthodox Jews around the world find the lack of recognition of their rabbis and institutions in Israel to be an intolerable situation. Reform Judaism must receive legal recognition in Israel and we must help the leaders of Israeli Reform Judaism press their case energetically. Our support is critically important to Reform congregations in Israel. Their vitality will be good for Israel's future. It will be good for us, too, because a strong Reform movement in Israel will have an increasingly positive impact on Reform congregations around the world. What is your congregation doing to realize these goals? What can your students do? How do your students react to the fact that Orthodox rabbis serving congregations in Israel are "official"—they can perform legal weddings, their salaries are paid by the government and they serve as chaplains in the Israel Defense Forces, while Reform, Conservative and Reconstructionist rabbis are denied these privileges and responsibilities?

CLASSROOM ENRICHMENT

1. What ritual objects/activities in your synagogue come from or deal with Israel? Some are discussed in Chapter Sixteen. Organize a "treasure hunt" for your students to see who can come up with the most Israel associations. (There should be many possibilities, some more obvious than others: Does the sanctuary face east? Does your synagogue sponsor trips to Israel? Has the congregation hosted visitors from your Federation's Project Renewal neighborhood, or from ARZA, Kibbutz Yahel, etc.? Are Israeli art, sculpture and/or ritual objects displayed in the congregation? Does the Judaica shop feature crafts, tallitot, etc. made in Israel? Do students in the Religious School have Israeli pen-pals? Do you march in an Israel Day parade or take part in community rallies? Did the congregation make a financial commitment to help resettle Ethiopian Jews in Israel? What about an Israeli flag? Classroom maps of Israel? Photographs?)

2. As evidenced in the establishment of Kibbutz Yahel (and now Kibbutz Lotan and the new settlement, Har Chalutz), Reform Judaism has made a definite commitment to Israel. Look with the class at the picture of the dedication ceremony for Kibbutz Yahel on page 147 in the textbook. Then constitute your students as the "members" of Kibbutz Yahel. Pose for them several problem situations on the order of the following: kashrut in public eating areas, public observance of Shabbat, the nature of permitted and prohibited work on Shabbat and festivals (do cows get milked? seedlings watered? ripe crops harvested?), acceptance or denial of membership to an intermarried couple (would the non-Jewish partner be a full member of the kibbutz?), etc. Ask the class to determine their course of action consistent with the principles of Reform Judaism.

BIOGRAPHY NOTEBOOK

As previous chapters have already indicated, the opposition to the upbuilding of the Jewish state was not the unanimous posture of Reform Jews. **Rabbi Abba Hillel Silver,** among others, was an important member of Zionist organizations and worked indefatigably on behalf of Israel. Enter his biography in the Notebook.

THINGS TO DO AT HOME

1. As an alternative or supplement to *Classroom Enrichment* #2 above, assign a student to write to Kibbutz Yahel and another to write to Kibbutz Lotan. Have them ask about the development of the kibbutz, where its members come from originally, how religious decisions are made, and any other questions that the student would like answered. The ARZA and WUPJ offices at the UAHC can probably help direct students' inquiries or perhaps answer all of their questions. At the same time, other students could write to HUC-JIR in Jerusalem in order to find out what students study there and why spending a year studying in Israel is so important to the training of Reform rabbis, cantors, and educators. Ask a few students, working together, to prepare a scrapbook on Har Chalutz, the first Reform *mitzpeh* in the Galilee. They should locate it on a map of Israel and include in their scrapbook as much as possible to help the class understand the liberal nature of the settlement and what makes it distinct from similar settlements. Other members of the class should be asked to find out all they can about the Reform synagogues in Israel. They, too, could contact the relevant offices at the UAHC.

2. Ask your students to write a brief essay on the subject, "What Israel means to me." Encourage them to share their essays in class.

17

Our Relation to the Jewish Community

FOCUS ON THE CHAPTER

Chapter Seventeen explores the relationship between the individual Jew and the community. "Community" is defined and described on many levels: "the Jews in your neighborhood or with whom your family associates; the members of your synagogue; all the Jews in your town; or all the people served by the agencies in your Federation; . . . all the Jews in America or even all the Jews in the world" (page 152).

APPROACHES

Since this chapter talks about many places across the globe, you will want to have a large world map in the classroom for this discussion. As you begin to talk about each area, pinpoint its location on the map. You may want to use glass tacks or similar pins to mark the spot. In that way, at the end of the discussion, it will be very obvious to your students how many different places matter to us because our brothers and sisters live there. The chapter also deals with many Jewish institutions (and their acronyms). It will simplify matters if you list the acronyms on the board or on a wall chart and write out the full names for each of the organizations. You may also want to use concentric circles—either drawn on the board or cut out of construction paper—to illustrate the overlapping (or, as the authors describe it, "nesting") relationship of the individual to the widening circles of community. As you work through the material in Chapter Seventeen, paragraph by paragraph, identify salient community elements as they are articulated in the text. It will be helpful to follow the suggestion made in the text and bring into class some copies of the local Anglo-Jewish newspaper in order to help explain and illustrate. Make reference to photographs, logos, short articles, editorials and the headings for the community service agencies.

You may also want to invite representatives from a few of the local organizations and local branches of national organizations to come and explain the purpose and function of their organization to your class. If your community has welcomed Jewish immigrants from various parts of the world, you may want to invite them to class, too, to share with your students stories about the country they have come from and the Jewish organizations like HIAS (mentioned in this chapter) that may have been of help to them in their journey here.

QUESTIONS FOR DISCUSSION

1. Chapter Seventeen concentrates on the relationship between individual Jews and the Jewish community. What ties—formal and informal—do your students have to the Jewish

community? What can your students, and their families, do for the community—from the synagogue level on up through world Jewry? Are some aspects of the Jewish community more important than others? Which is the most important?

2. Present to your students the following situation: The class has just completed a campaign to raise funds for hunger relief. They have raised $100 and are debating where the money should go. Two organizations approach them with requests for the money. One is the hunger drive launched by a group of rock stars; the other is the social action office of the UAHC. To whom should the class contribute the money? Why? If it is to be divided, how—and why?

3. After discussing the goals of some of the organizations in Chapter Seventeen that are designed to help Jews, guide the class into coming up with a list of activities that students can do to express their solidarity with endangered Jews throughout the world. Ask each student to make a commitment to one such activity. To help direct them, you might want to contact the National Conference on Soviet Jewry (or one of the other organizations active on behalf of Soviet Jews) and ask them for the profile of a refusenik family with whom your class could correspond. A member of the local Soviet Jewry committee should be happy to come and give the class an update on the Soviet Jewry situation and make clear to the class why it is indeed a mitzvah to maintain contact with these brave Jews.

CLASSROOM ENRICHMENT

1. In some of the largest cities in this country, there is a full range of Jewish community organizations. They care for individual needs, from childcare through facilities for the elderly and Jewish burial societies; watch out for the welfare of the local Jewish community and the needs of Jews on the national level and around the world; provide educational, cultural and recreational facilities. Many regions, however, are not so fortunate. Invite a professional from your local Federation to talk to the class about the services and agencies available in your community (the constituent agencies of the Federation as well as those that are not affiliated with the federated community) and to share with the students a sense of what the community lacks. To prepare for this visit, assign students to write to the various national organizations listed in Chapter Seventeen. They can find the addresses in the *American Jewish Yearbook* (issued each year by the American Jewish Committee and published by the Jewish Publication Society). Find out what their stated goals are. How do they impact on the life of Jews in your community? Discuss these in class. Make a comparison chart on the board in order to determine if these organizations do some of the same things. Discuss why that could be a problem, and also why there are advantages to more than one group dealing with the same problems and expressing public opinions on the same issues.

2. The local Jewish community newspaper is a means of communication for the communal structure. Get multiple copies of one issue. In order to help them understand the way a newspaper works, "walk" your students through the various categories in an issue of the Jewish community newspaper. Then, have the students prepare a "sample" issue of the Jewish community's newspaper, including in it information—real or imaginary—about local Jewish agencies and important events. It should reflect their understanding of what the community is and how it functions.

3. Invite a local member of AIPAC, the American Israel Public Affairs Committee, to class to speak to your students about how to respond to anti-Israel propaganda.

4. As a concluding exercise for this chapter, ask students to describe their vision of the perfect Jewish community. Where would all of the people live? What buildings/organizations would be necessary? Remind the class, if they haven't taken these things into account, about the needs of the elderly, the disadvantaged, the ill, the requirements for day care and resettling of immigrants, etc. Have they allowed for the range of religious observance and provided for it? What about leisure time activities? Dissemination of news? Cultural programming? Have they remembered to watch out for the safety of the community—or to reach beyond the Jewish community in order to offer help during crises, and to participate in ongoing interfaith and interracial activities? Will they concern themselves with Israel? World Jewry? How do they anticipate funding it all? As they cannot help but realize, the Jewish community is a very complex intersection of organizations, structures and needs.

BIOGRAPHY NOTEBOOK

David Phillipson, a member of the first graduating class of Hebrew Union College, was instrumental in many aspects of the developing Reform movement in America. To this day, his book called *The Reform Movement in Judaism* remains indispensable for anyone studying the classical period of Reform Judaism. Prepare his biography for the notebook.

THING TO DO AT HOME

1. Have students discuss with their families the nature of their involvement with the organizations and agencies in the local and national Jewish community structure. What motivates them to participate? To contribute time and money?

2. Have students collect pictures, brochures and articles about the organizations in the community and use them to make a collage. Ask the students to bring them to class. Display their work in the classroom and in the school corridor.

18

Reaching Out to Our Country and the World

FOCUS ON THE CHAPTER

Reform Judaism's commitment to universal ethics, its emphasis on improving the human condition, includes a call to action against injustice—in the United States and around the world. Chapter Eighteen calls attention, through text and photographs, to a number of Americans whose Jewish sense of justice prompted them to take action. As an extension of this commitment to universal ethics, Reform Jews have made a conscious effort to be involved in the democratic process. The best summary for this chapter appears in its final paragraph, as an explication of the famous dictum of Hillel: "A mature Jewish religious life demands concern for ourselves and others—particularism and universalism—and requires action on behalf of both." "If I am not for myself, who will be for me? If I am only for myself, what kind of person am I?"

APPROACHES

This is the last substantive chapter prior to the conclusion of the text. Begin with a quick chronological review of the situation of the Jewish community in the colonial and early national periods of this country's history. Next, discuss with the class the illustrations on page 161. What Jonas Phillips did was a very small act, but it is indicative of the Jewish attitude toward just causes. Commodore Levy was instrumental in changing conditions for a great many people. Many young people might find it difficult to understand why anyone would wish to serve in the military. It is necessary, therefore, to help them see the importance of Asser Levy's insistence on serving in the militia. "Justice for all" involves having everyone play a role in society. Full civic responsibility, the text points out, is something Jews take very seriously.

Review with the class the relationship between the American democratic process and the freedom of choice so important to Reform Judaism. There are many different ways in which we, as individual Jews and Americans, can express our rights. The important thing, as the chapter says, is to be knowledgeable and to be involved. "The New 'Commandments' That Came with Democracy," and "How Much Leadership Should Government Exercise?" (pages 163–165) deal with these issues.

On pages 165–166, the text mentions a broad range of areas outside the political process where the help of ethical, caring and responsible individuals continues to be vitally necessary. "Judaism doesn't want *martyrs* for ethical progress—but all of us now or later should use our influence for the universal good." Spend some time on this point with the class, because it is not an easy one. You might want to make reference to people who went on freedom marches for civil rights in the South during the early 1960s, perhaps citing the case of Goodman,

Schwerner, and Chaney, young students who were murdered for their efforts. Jews have always been disproportionately involved in activism on behalf of the human rights of others. Have your students look back to pages 125–129 in Chapter Fourteen for some reminders of why this is so. Also note that activism on behalf of the rights of others can take place at home, as it were, "in your clubs and associations" (page 165). That it is not an easy job does not absolve us of the obligation to continue "trying to apply our ethical standards to the world as a whole" (page 166).

Conclude your study of the chapter (pages 165–168) within the framework of Hillel's famous quotation (in the last paragraph of the chapter). Organize a debate between groups of your students on the question of particularism vs. universalism. Analyze the problems with the old Reform notions of the "mission of Israel" and our obligation to be a "light to the nations." And yet, they were noble goals. Elaborate on the need for balancing particularist Jewish needs with universalist goals—for both selfish and altruistic reasons. "If not now," as the chapter concludes, "when?"

QUESTIONS FOR DISCUSSION

1. Reform Judaism insists that the privilege of free choice belongs to everyone. In this context, explore with your students the following question: Would Reform Judaism be possible in a totalitarian society?
2. Our country is committed to the total separation of church and state. Is that always a good thing? Does it always work? In what specific ways does maintaining this separation affect the Jewish community—negatively as well as positively? Use examples relating to Christmas observances, prayer in school, holiday closings, and quotas. On balance, students should conclude that as a small minority group, we Jews have more to gain by the separation of church and state than by living in a theocracy.

CLASSROOM ENRICHMENT

1. What does Hillel's statement, in the last sentences of Chapter Eighteen, mean in practical terms? Can the class devise a plan for their own ethical behavior and commitment to social action?

THINGS TO DO AT HOME

1. Have students ask family members about their past and present involvement in social issues and on the political scene. What should they learn from what they hear?

2. Before this session of the class, ascertain some of the issues likely to be on local, state or national election ballots this year. Assign individual students different issues and have each one prepare a Jewish position on the subject he/she has been given. Encourage them to ask their parents' advice.

Part 5
In Closing

FOCUS

Read page 169 to the class or ask a student to read it aloud. This introduction to the final chapter of the text is really an introduction to the reality of Jewish life. Beyond the peaks and valleys, the roller coaster of human existence, is an eternal hope for the future.

CONTEST #5

"How my favorite superhero might try to bring about the messianic age." Here's an example:

Clark Kent walked dejectedly through the poorest neighborhood in town. He kicked broken glass out of his path and barely avoided being kicked himself as two drunks lurched after a big, ugly gray rat. "It isn't fair," he thought. "There's so much misery here while over on the other side of town some evil rich merchants are overcharging their customers and cheating the government. This calls for a superhuman effort. This calls for Superman." He began looking around for a phone booth, but it seemed that the city didn't trust the neighborhood enough to put phone booths there. Finally he found one. All of the glass had been knocked out of the panes and the phone itself ripped off the wall, but it was a phone booth all right. He brushed aside the empty liquor bottles and, holding his breath. . .

19
Our Hope for the Messianic Age

FOCUS ON THE CHAPTER

This chapter outlines the nature of Jewish hope, expressed as messianism or a belief in a messianic age. Chapter Nineteen presents the traditional Jewish vision of the Messiah and how this vision conflicts with Christianity, past and present. The text moves on to explain that Reform Judaism had problems with the traditional notion of a Messiah in Judaism, but did not discard the basic concept. The Reformers restructured the idea (see pages 173–174). The early Reformers had great faith in the potential of humankind to wipe out evil in the world. In more recent decades, however, both liberal and and traditional Jews have become, for sad reasons, more realistic about human potential to do evil. And yet, we must do what we can. We are partners with God, who guides our power to do good. A good and honorable life, for us and for future generations, is what our Jewish quest is all about.

APPROACHES

It will be important for students to read this chapter completely several different times in different contexts. The material is extremely important and relevant, but conceptually difficult. Work through the chapter methodically, section by section. Begin by discussing the traditional notion of Messiah in Judaism. Using a giant card or the blackboard, list all of the characteristics of a Messiah. Familiarity with the traditional Jewish concept of Messiah is indispensable to an understanding of the material presented in the remainder of the chapter. Duplicate for the class copies of Isaiah 7:14 or Isaiah 53. These are commonly used as proof texts by Christian missionaries. Show the students how these passages are misinterpreted by proselytizers. The textbook, pages 171–173, should be of help in this.

For the next section, pages 173–174, ask your students if either the Christian idea of Messiah or the traditional Jewish messianic idea is acceptable to them. Using the remainder of the chapter as a guide, deal with the Reform movement's reaction to traditional messianism and with the world events that have shaped the Reform response, especially the two key events of the second half of this century, the Holocaust and the birth of the State of Israel.

Conclude your study of the chapter (and the book) by reading together the Aleinu (Adoration) and the passages that conclude it in *Gates of Prayer*.

QUESTIONS FOR DISCUSSION

1. The Reform Jewish idea of messianism differs from that of traditional Judaism, as explained in Chapter Nineteen. Discuss some of the differences. As a follow-up to *Things*

to Do at Home, discuss the messianic aspects of the Bar Kokhbah rebellion or the case of Shabbetai Zevi.

2. Can people's need for messianic answers lead them to believe in leaders who do not relate in any way to the traditional vision of a Messiah? What about Hitler, or Mussolini, or the Ayatollah Khomeini? What kinds of needs lead people to long for a messianic solution?

CLASSROOM ENRICHMENT

1. Ask the class what Christians who use Isaiah 7:14 and Isaiah 53 as prooftexts are actually suggesting? Look at pages 172–173 for the relevant information. Would they make their claim as strongly if the texts were not there? With student input, prepare a booklet of responses to the Christian claim that Jesus is the Messiah. Or, prepare an "evidence box" that contains items controverting Christian claims that the Messiah has come. Include evidence that our world is still far from the perfection we hope for.

2. Do your students think that modern Reform Jews are working toward a messianic era? How? Ask students to discuss in practical terms the messianic hopes of their generation. Have students respond in writing to the question of whether they believe in messianism (and why). How do they envision the messianic era?

3. Ask students to write their own ending for the sentence in the middle of page 176 (the final paragraph of the Adoration): "We therefore hope, O Lord, Our God, soon to behold . . ."

THINGS TO DO AT HOME

1. Assign students research reports on two who briefly raisemd Jewish messianic hopes, Bar Kokhbah and Shabbetai Zevi. Have them share their findings with the class.

Concluding Exercises

1. Help the class select the ten most important dates in the history of Reform Judaism. Students must give reasons for their choices—and you should be prepared to redirect the class' selections if you feel that they have not properly understood what is key to the development of the Reform movement and the Reform Jewish way of looking at the world. The purpose of this exercise is twofold: it should serve as a review of the entire course and should also put the concerns and emphases of the Reform movement into proper perspective.

2. Ask students to write their own conclusion for this textbook—an "afterword" or "afterthought," based on what they have learned about Reform Judaism. How has this course changed their view of Reform Judaism, their view of themselves as Reform Jews, and their outlook on life?

Biography Notebook Assignment Record

Chapter	Name of Biographical Entry	Student assigned
1	Moses Mendelssohn Israel Jacobson	
2	Leopold Zunz Abraham Geiger	
3	Gustav Poznanski Isaac Mayer Wise	
4	Zacharias Frankel	
5	Stephen S. Wise	
6	David Einhorn	
7	Leo Baeck	
8	Samuel Hirsch	
9	Nelson Glueck Israel Mattuck	
10	Eugene Borowitz Martin Buber	
11	Bernhard Felsenthal Judah Magnes	
12	Julian Morgenstern	
13	Maurice Eisendrath Emil Hirsch	
14	Lillian Helen Montagu	
15	Kaufmann Kohler Jacob Z. Lauterbach	
16	Abba Hillel Silver	
17	David Phillipson	

Capsule Biographies

With one notable exception, the following biographical entries are about people no longer alive. For the present generation of Reform leadership, whose careers are far from over, we wish many more years of fruitful work, and we leave their biographies to future generations of students. The one exception is Rabbi Eugene Borowitz, who, as co-author of the *Explaining Reform Judaism,* holds special interest to students of *this* generation.

Most of these biographical entries include quotations from the speeches and writings of the person described. The quotations were reproduced in and have been taken from one or another of three different sources: Gunter Plaut's two volumes, *The Rise of Reform Judaism* and *The Growth of Reform Judaism*; Marc Lee Raphael's *Profiles in American Judaism*; and Sylvan Schwartzman's *Reform Judaism Then and Now.* These sources are all fully identified in our bibliography.

LEO BAECK (1874–1956), a rabbi and theologian, was the spiritual guide and exemplar for the Jews incarcerated in the Nazi "show" camp called Terezin—and, when the story became known, to an entire generation of Jews. He was born in Germany and studied there. In the 1920s, he became head of the Reform rabbinical seminary. He was elected head of the organization of German Jewry in the early 1930s (when Hitler first came to power). Although he could have emigrated, he chose to stay with the German Jewish community and was ultimately sent to Terezin. He survived the Holocaust and, after the liberation of the camps, went to England where he became president of the World Union for Progressive Judaism. In his first address to this group, in 1946, he shared the insights he had learned while in the concentration camp. He did not look back or dwell on the horror, nor did he ask where was God. Instead, he looked to the future. He expressed his excitement that "in Eretz Yisrael, a Jewish life of our own is blossoming. . . . In all our grief, we may feel grateful too." He urged the unflagging commitment of liberal/progressive Jews to the concept of "K'lal Yisrael."

EUGENE BOROWITZ (1924–   ), besides being a co-author of our text, is professor of Education and Jewish Religious Thought at Hebrew Union College-Jewish Institute of Religion (HUC-JIR) in New York, and editor of *Sh'ma: A Journal of Jewish Responsibility.* Perhaps the foremost theologian in the Reform movement, he chaired the Central Conference of American Rabbis' (CCAR) committee that prepared the Centenary Perspective (1976). In his theological teaching and writings, Rabbi Borowitz emphasizes a personal God with whom people come to have give-and-take, "I-Thou" relationships. God "hears us," Borowitz says, and "we must therefore learn to care about Him and base our lives on the intimacy we share with Him."

MARTIN BUBER (1878–1965) was born in Vienna and lived for many years in Frankfurt, Germany. His work as a philosopher and theologian (the concept of "I-Thou" and "I-It" relationships between human beings as well as between human beings and God was developed by Buber) influenced not only modern Judaism but also Christian religious thinking. He was active in the renewal of *Wissenschaft des Judenthums* in the years following

80

the First World War. Together with Franz Rosenzweig, he translated the Bible into German. He also did a lot of work in hasidic literature, and made the insights of Hasidism appealing to liberal Jews. Buber was also a Zionist thinker and leader. In 1938, he fled Germany and went to Palestine, where he became a professor at Hebrew University.

DAVID EINHORN (1809–1879) was born in Bavaria. He was already an outspoken radical reformer by the time he came to Har Sinai congregation in Baltimore, in 1855. In this country, he became the chief spokesman for the most extreme, uncompromising reforms of his day and was therefore at odds with the positions advanced by Isaac M. Wise. In his first sermon in America, Einhorn condemned the "futility of lifeless religious practices." He began publishing a periodical he called *Sinai* (in German) to counter Wise's weekly, *Israelite,* which he regarded as too conservative and too willing to compromise with tradition. (Yet throughout his life, he continued to wear a kippah and a tallit during services, and was a strict observer of Shabbat.) Einhorn's prayer book, *Olath Tamid,* first published in 1858 (in Hebrew and German, and then, later, in Hebrew and English), became the basis for the first *Union Prayerbook* (rather than its chief competitor, Wise's *Minhag America*). Einhorn was an outspoken opponent of slavery and secession and was forced to leave Baltimore for his own physical safety. He settled first in Philadelphia and then in New York. Emil Hirsch and Kaufmann Kohler, two of the outstanding Reform rabbis of the next generation, were his sons-in-law.

MAURICE EISENDRATH (1902–1973) was president of the Union of American Hebrew Congregations (UAHC) from 1943–1973. Rabbi Eisendrath was strongly committed to living the ethical concepts so important to Reform Judaism and devoted much of his energies to social action: bettering interfaith relations and achieving fair civil rights legislation. He urged all Reform Jews to work together, in congregations and through the organizations of the movement, "to apply the precepts and practices of prophetic Jewish faith in combating all forms of injustice and bigotry."

BERNHARD FELSENTHAL (1822–1908) was born in Germany and came to America in 1854. In this country he became the first rabbi of the Sinai congregation in Chicago (1861). He believed passionately in the "mission" of Reform to work toward that "distant future in which the whole of mankind will unite in a single grand temple of God." He was also a strong—and very early—Reform advocate of Zionism. (Most Reformers didn't come to share his views for almost fifty years.) He believed that the end result of opposition to a Jewish State would be assimilation, and "assimilation leads . . . to total annihilation of Israel" [the *people* as well as the homeland]. In the June 1890 issue of *The Menorah* (a magazine sponsored by B'nai B'rith), Rabbi Felsenthal wrote: "We need but state that a Jew is a Jew in consequence of his birth, or in consequence of his formal application and adoption, and that he remains a Jew as long as he does not openly and unmistakably separate himself from the Jewish community." For Rabbi Felsenthal, self-identification as a Jew was sufficient qualification for Jewishness.

ZACHARIAS FRANKEL (1801–1875) was born in Prague. He was a noted scholar of his time and became head of the Breslau Juedisch-Theologisches Seminary [the Breslau Jewish Theological Seminary], the first modern German rabbinical school. He wrote, "We shall conceive it to be our task to avoid the kind of negative reform which leads to complete dissolution, but instead, to show how the teachings of Judaism itself contain the possibility of progress." He was strongly opposed to radical reform, and is considered the spiritual father of the Conservative movement of today.

ABRAHAM GEIGER (1810–1874) was probably the most influential rabbi and leader of Reform Judaism in Europe. Very early in his career, he came up against Solomon Titkin, the chief rabbi in Breslau, whose assistant he became. Titkin opposed all of Geiger's ideas and, ultimately, took him to court to try to prevent him from retaining his position and instituting innovations. All of Western European Jewry took sides in the battle. When Geiger won the right to retain his position, it was a turning point for Reform. In 1870, Geiger published a prayer book in Berlin. It removed the "national" elements, which he saw as anachronistic in a "universal" Reform service, specifically the "separation of Israel and the other peoples, which . . . has no right to be expressed in prayer." It looked to the "unification of all mankind" and deleted the restoration of a Jewish State, the rebuilding of the Temple, the ingathering of exiles, etc., concepts, he felt, that were "wholly faded from our consciousness." In another area, he made clear that in Reform Judaism "there be from now on no distinctions and duties for men and women." Yet he also believed in moderation: "Revolution is not successful in religion, which demands not only tearing away whatever is outmoded but strengthening that which exists and creating new things when necessity demands it." One of the early reformers, he wanted Reform to remain part of Judaism, not become a separate religion.

NELSON GLUECK (1900–1971) was a native of Cincinnati who, like many of his contemporaries, went to Germany to study, earning his doctorate in 1927. In the 1930s and 40s, he was director of the American School of Oriental Research in Jerusalem, and from 1942–47 of the American School of Oriental Research in Baghdad. He was already a famous biblical archeologist when he was invited to become president of Hebrew Union College (HUC). Glueck was the first president of Hebrew Union College-Jewish Institute of Religion, the new Reform rabbinical school created when he effected the merger of HUC (in Cincinnati) with the Jewish Institute of Religion (JIR) in New York City. As Gunther Plaut describes it, "the merger heralded a new era in the development of the movement—the liberal spirit of Judaism represented by [HUC's] founder Isaac M. Wise reacquiring the full force of Jewish peoplehood represented by Stephen Wise [founder of JIR]. The merger brought the period of Reform's radicalism decisively to a close." Nelson Glueck served as president until his death. During that time, the faculty rose from 12 full-time teachers (between the two schools) to 40, the student body doubled, and campuses were established in Los Angeles and in Jerusalem.

EMIL HIRSCH (1851–1923) was an American-born rabbi, the son of Samuel Hirsch (and son-in-law of David Einhorn). He was a fighter for social reforms and helped establish various welfare organizations in Chicago; he was a scholar, who taught at the University of Chicago, which he helped found; and he was a leader of the radical wing of Reform Judaism. He was also an extraordinarily eloquent preacher. He served as rabbi of the Sinai Congregation in Chicago. His Judaism was radically focused on the ethical aspects of Judaism as opposed to all halakhic concerns. He believed that "ethical monotheism is the original and the essential content of Judaism. . . . Not the Law [i.e., the Torah], then, but the Prophetic principles constitute the essence of Judaism. He was one of the only rabbis who would not put a Torah scroll in the ark of his congregation, because he did not consider it sacred! He stated his approach to Judaism proudly, "I [am] the Minister of a Radical Reform congregation. . . . now the younger men [meaning American born and/or trained rabbis like himself] have come; they speak English [rather than German] and dare to follow the bold example of Einhorn, dare to be aggressive." Emil Hirsch was also a leading proponent of Sunday services, and pioneered a Sunday Sabbath at Sinai Congregation.

SAMUEL HIRSCH (1815–1889) was born in Germany. He was influential in formulating the philosophy of the radical wing of the Reform movement—at first in Germany and, later, in America, where he was rabbi of Keneseth Israel in Philadelphia (after David Einhorn). Hirsch was one of the founders of the Wissenschaft des Judentums. At the age of 26, he published *Religious Philosophy of Jewry,* a brilliant application of the philosophy of Hegel to Judaism. Before coming to the United States, he served as Chief Rabbi of the Grand Duchy of Luxembourg. During that time, he engaged in a public controversy with Zacharias Frankel about the nature of Reform. His criticisms of traditional Judaism were the careful conclusions of a man who took his "scientific endeavors" (*wissenschaft*) seriously: "I have always sought to evaluate every event in the area of religion in its historical importance."

ISRAEL JACOBSON (1768–1828), a prominent German financier and philanthropist, was one of the founders of Reform Judaism. His innovations included shortened religious services, regular sermons preached in the vernacular, the use of an organ and mixed choir, and the institution of Confirmation. The co-educational, Jewish/secular school he founded in Seesen, Westphalia, remained in existence until the 1930s. Like Jacobson, the other earliest leaders of the Reform movement (Jacob Herz Beer, for example) were businessmen who wished to create a "modern," rational, non-particularist, esthetically attractive and "enlightened" way of *remaining* Jewish. They provided their energy, their funds and even their homes in order to hold worship services and amend their Jewish practices in order to satisfy these needs. Jacobson's speech at the dedication of the synagogue in his school at Seesen (1810) spells out their desires: "What I had in mind when I first thought about building this temple was *your* religious education, my Israelite brothers, *your* customs, *your* worship. Be it far from me that I should have any secret intention to undermine the pillars of your faith, to diminish our old and honored principles through the glitter of new opinions, or that, because of some hidden vanity, I should become a traitor to both our religion and you. You know my faithful adherence to the faith of my fathers. I need not protest it. My actions will witness for me more than my words. But . . . On all sides, enlightenment opens up new areas for development. Why should we alone remain behind?"

KAUFMANN KOHLER (1843–1926) was born in Germany. He studied with Samson Raphael Hirsch, the founder of neo-Orthodoxy, who influenced him greatly. He was also much influenced by Abraham Geiger. After he came to America, Kohler married David Einhorn's daughter, and espoused much of Einhorn's thinking. Kaufmann Kohler was the "leading theoretician of classical Reform" (Plaut). In 1885, Kohler convened the conference in Pittsburgh and drafted the radical positions presented in the platform. (Only 20 rabbis participated in this conference, whose platform directed mainstream Reform thinking for some fifty years! Their deliberations were, in part, a response to the alarming appeal of Felix Adler's Ethical Culture Society, many of whose adherents were drawn from the Reform Jewish community.) In 1903, Kohler became president of the Reform rabbinical school, Hebrew Union College, and continued in that position until 1921. He was a militant anti-Zionist; he also opposed the ceremony of bar mitzvah: "Disregarding altogether the false claim of mental maturity of the thirteen-year-old boy for a true realization of life's sacred obligations, I maintain that the bar mitzvah rite ought not to be encouraged by any Reform rabbi, as it is a survival of orientalism like the covering of the head during the service, whereas the confirmation—when made as it should, by the rabbi, an impressive appeal to the holiest emotions of the soul and as personal vow of fealty to the ancestral faith—is a source of regeneration of Judaism each year, the value of which none who has the spiritual welfare of Israel at heart can afford to underrate or to ignore."

JACOB Z. LAUTERBACH (1873–1942) was born in Galicia and immigrated to the United States in 1903. He was a talmudic scholar and served as a member of the faculty of HUC from 1911 to 1934. For many years he chaired the Responsa Committee of the CCAR. Among his responsa was one permitting the use of birth control ("as based upon a correct understanding of the halachic teachings of the Talmud as accepted by the medieval rabbinic authorities"), and another opposing the ordination of women, which he held to be "not merely a question of liberalism" but to be unnecessarily "acting contrary to the very spirit of traditional Judaism which the Rabbinate seeks to uphold and preserve. . . . Shall we adhere to the tradition or shall we separate ourselves from Catholic Israel [k'lal yisrael] and introduce a radical innovation which would necessarily create a distinction between the title Rabbi, as held by a Reform Rabbi, and the title Rabbi in general." (The CCAR voted, in spite of his responsum, in favor of the principle of ordaining women—although a great many years passed before Jewish women, influenced by the women's liberation movement, made any serious efforts to pursue rabbinic ordination.) Lauterbach's responsum about kippah-wearing, showing that it hadn't "always" been done—was much quoted as individual congregations struggled with the forms of traditional practice.

JUDAH MAGNES (1877–1948) was an American-born Reform rabbi whose communal and Zionist interest occupied most of his life. He was the organizer and guiding light of the New York Jewish Kehillah during its entire existence (1908–1922). He was responsible for the formation of the Joint Distribution Committee and for the Yiddish daily newspaper, *Der Tog*. He moved to Palestine where he helped found the Hebrew University, became its Chancellor in 1925 and, in 1938, moved from that post to become its first president. He favored the establishment of Israel as a bi-national state and worked very hard to better relations between Jews and Arabs. He vehemently fought against the anti-Zionism of many Reform Jews and tried to convince the movement to give more emphasis to the teaching of Hebrew in religious schools. He wrote, "I would rather be a Jew writing in Hebrew against a reconstructed Jewish theology, than be of these modern priests of the Lord who prate their Judaism saving the world, but who do not understand how integral a part of our life is our national language."

ISRAEL MATTUCK (1883–1954) was born in Lithuania and received his rabbinic ordination at HUC. From 1912, he served as rabbi of the Liberal Jewish Synagogue in London. He was among the people responsible for creating the World Union for Progressive Judaism. He believed that Judaism should seek to attract converts. As such, he was a strong proponent of universalism: "For the synagogues to exercise a missionary function, they must give their Services a universal form. The adherence of Judaism to ancient and antiquated observances has evoked the accusation that it is 'fossilized' or 'stagnant.' The accusation is not true, but the fact that it is made points to a misunderstanding of its nature produced by the stress on old forms which have no obvious religious significance in the modern world."

MOSES MENDELSSOHN (1729–1786) was one of a number of successful Jewish businessmen in Berlin who had business dealings with non-Jews even before the Emancipation. The son of a pious family in Dessau, Germany, he did not grow up speaking German (his native language was Yiddish), yet he mastered German so thoroughly that he became a leading writer of essays in German clarifying what made good and bad German writing styles! He came to believe that all German Jews could live according to traditional Jewish law and at the same time follow modern German customs and styles, as he was doing. The major barrier standing in the way, he felt, was that Jews didn't know German. So he translated the Torah into German, hoping that by comparing the Hebrew text—with which most Jews were familiar—

to the German, they could soon learn the new language. But the Jewish leadership forbade anyone to read his translation. They were afraid that cross-cultural contacts would lead Jews to leave Judaism. Actually, very few Jews were personally comfortable with Mendelssohn's way of combining Judaism and contemporary civilization. Most felt it was wrong for people to split themselves into two separate parts—one strictly Jewish, the other entirely modern. That was the "both at one time" problem the texts talks about (see pages 5–6). In fact, by the early 1800s, all of Mendelssohn's own grandchildren had made their choice and converted to Christianity. Mendelssohn's response to the Emancipation was a brave try, but ultimately a failure.

LILLIAN (LILY) HELEN MONTAGU (1873–1963) was a founder of the Jewish Liberal Union in England and one of its lay preachers. A social worker and magistrate by profession, she was very instrumental in creating the World Union for Progressive Judaism. For many years she served as its Honorary Secretary and later became its president. In her remarks to the International Conference of Liberal Jews, which created the World Union for Progressive Judaism, Lily Montagu envisioned the role of the World Union as a "global messenger" showing "How Judaism makes for justice, righteousness and peace today, even as it did hundreds of years ago."

JULIAN MORGENSTERN (1881–1976) was born in America. He was a Bible scholar who served as professor of Bible at HUC from 1907 until 1922, when he was named president of the School. (He was the last president of HUC before its merger with JIR.) He championed higher biblical criticism—"Biblical science," as he termed it—and was emphatic in his assertion that "Biblical Science is not destructive at all, but thoroughly constructive. It does not uproot the foundations of religious belief, as so many think. . . . Rather it has given the old Bible back to us, re-interpreted and with larger message and deeper and more eternal significance than ever before." During the 1930s, Rabbi Morgenstern was instrumental in bringing five of the students at the German liberal seminary (the Hochschule fur Wissenschaft des Judentums) to HUC, thus saving them from almost certain death. He also gave employment to twelve other Jewish scholars from Germany. Marc Raphael writes, "This generous act of salvation, which came at great expense to the college, was remembered by some as Morgenstern's most important single effort."

DAVID PHILIPSON (1862–1949) was a member of the first rabbinical school class ordained at HUC. He was the rabbi of KK Bene Israel in Cincinnati for some fifty years. He was an important influence on the CCAR and the direction of the Reform movement. His book, *The Reform Movement in Judaism,* is the clearest exposition of the classical Reform position. He was the co-author of the Pittsburgh Platform (and called for the adoption of the Columbus Platform, even though he had not seen the need for the changes it made and did not agree with many of them). Philipson was the first to call for raising the age for confirmation—"the older the better, for then there is more possibility of a proper comprehension of the instruction." He wrote: "every rabbi who has had confirmation classes under his instruction has felt that the age of thirteen, or even fourteen, is entirely too early for a proper comprehension of the lessons taught, and also that however deep may be the impression made on the day of confirmation the children are not old enough for a proper appreciation of the meaning and importance of the ceremony. We should not have an age test, but a capability test. In the first place, no child that has not taken the full course of the Sabbath-school instruction should be permitted to enter the confirmation class."

GUSTAV POZNANSKI (1805–1879) was a Polish Jew who was educated in Hamburg,

Germany. He came to Charleston, South Carolina, and became the leader of the Beth Elohim congregation. He was trained as a cantor, not a rabbi, but was better qualified to fill the position than anyone else there at the time. Although it had been founded as a Orthodox congregation, various reforms and modifications were introduced. When their new religious leader arrived, the congregation was already using an organ (on alternate weeks), had a shortened worship service and made the request that Poznanski preach in English. The congregation was a first step in the development of a Reform movement in America. At the 1841 dedication of Beth Elohim's new building, Poznanski declared "this synagogue is our *temple*, this city our *Jerusalem*, this happy land our *Palestine*, and as our fathers defended with their lives *that* temple, *that* city and *that* land, so will their sons defend *this* temple, *this* city, and *this* land. . . ." It was while attending a debate involving Poznanski (and Rabbi Morris Raphall) that I.M. Wise made his statement about a personal messiah and the resurrection of the dead—leading to the fist fight and split in his own congregation that year.

ABBA HILLEL SILVER (1893–1963) came to America from Lithuania. He was ordained by Hebrew Union College. In 1917 he became rabbi of The Temple (Tifereth Israel) in Cleveland, Ohio and remained in that position until his death. He was a brilliant orator and a fighter for social causes—particularly in the city where he spent so much of his life. He spoke of the Reform movement's commitment to "unremitting action" and "unwearied moral effort" to "build the good society" and acted upon his words. Rabbi Silver was a key Zionist leader. Gunther Plaut says he "has been called the chief architect of the State of Israel." He was head of the United Palestine Appeal (a forerunner of the UJA) and the American Section of the Jewish Agency. He presented the case for an independent Jewish State to the United Nations General Assembly in 1947. (See the photograph on page 97 of the text.) Silver was very instrumental in shifting the Reform rabbinate from its anti-Zionist position to one favoring the creation of a Jewish State in Palestine. (He was also a prominently identified Republican at a time when most American Jews were members of the Democratic Party.)

ISAAC MAYER WISE (1819–1900), known as the "father of American Reform," was born in Bohemia and came to America in 1846. His background was traditional and he apparently moved slowly at first in making changes in his first pulpit, the Beth El congregation in Albany, New York. Within a few years, however, (after the famous Rosh Hashanah battle of 1850), he and his supporters had left Beth El and formed the first Reform congregation in Albany, Anshe Emeth. From there he went to Cincinnati, where he was again hired by a traditional congregation, Bene Yeshurun (today more commonly known as the Plum Street Temple). Over the years he initiated mixed seating, a late service on Friday and all of the other innovations that marked the congregation as clearly Reform. He was a brilliant and visionary leader and organizer. He founded, wrote and edited the *Israelite,* an English language weekly (whose name was changed to *American Israelite* in 1874). He was very concerned both about uniting the Jewish community and Americanizing it.

STEPHEN S. WISE (1874–1949) was born in Hungary. Although he and I.M. Wise had the same last name, they were not related. They had much in common, however, since Stephen Wise was as much a guide and shining light to his contemporaries as the earlier Wise had been to his. Rabbi Stephen Wise was a social and political activist, a spellbinding orator and an indefatigable champion of Zionist causes. He was a founder and first secretary of the Federation of American Zionists (which became the Zionist Organization of America), was American Secretary for the World Zionist movement, head of the Provisional Committee for Zionist affairs (1916–19) and was a founder and president of the American Jewish Congress. As president of the American Jewish Congress, he was one of the Jewish leaders who in the late 1930s and early 1940s attempted (unsuccessfully, for the most part) to pursue more active efforts on behalf of Jews trapped in Nazi Europe. Wise insisted on freedom of the pulpit—the right of a rabbi to speak out on controversial issues without congregational censorship. For that reason, he refused the invitation to become rabbi of Temple Emanu-El in New York, which did not wish to extend such freedom. In 1922, he also founded a rabbinical school in New York: the Jewish Institute of Religion, which trained rabbis to serve either Reform or Conservative congregations. In the last year of his life, he helped guide the merger of J.I.R. with Hebrew Union College.

LEOPOLD ZUNZ (1794–1886) was born in 1794. Both of his parents died when he was still very young. Soon after their death he was given a scholarship to attend a modern Jewish school of the sort that Israel Jacobson was developing. Zunz grew up prepared to believe that it was possible to be fully modern and fully Jewish at the same time—only no one yet knew exactly how that might be done.

He was the first Jew in the town of Wolfenbuttel, Germany, to go to high school rather than pursuing a yeshiva-type education. He then attended the University of Berlin and finally received his Ph.D. from the University of Halle, in 1821. Since Jewish studies were not offered in any colleges in those days, he worked on his own, using the study methods he was learning in his regular university courses to analyze the Jewish material.

He and the handful of other Jewish students interested in learning about Judaism realized that they had to find a modern way of studying the tradition. They called for a "science" of Judaism, a new Jewish research method that would examine Jewish documents with the critical thoroughness used in every other intellectual field. Zunz alone went on to show what the "science" of Judaism might be like. He did so in the preparation of his case regarding Jewish sermons.

He believed that *midrash* represented the sermon-giving of earlier generations, and that the midrash books were in fact collections of old Jewish sermons that had been preached in ancient synagogues. His task was to prove that midrashim were indeed sermons and that sermons had continued to be preached in synagogues for hundreds of years after the time of the Talmud. The book he finally wrote when he finished his research was called *The Historical Development of the Jewish Sermon*. It appeared nine years after the closing of the Beer Temple, in 1832. (The German title is *Die gottesdienstliche Vortraege der Juden historisch entwickelt*—literally, "the religious-service discourses of the Jews, historically developed.") It is an incredible tribute to his intelligence, his mastery of the techniques and sources and the extent of evidence with which he backed his conclusions that no one in the more than 150 years since he wrote has needed to refute him. His book still stands as the authority on the subject.

In fact, today, all modern study of Judaism is done Zunz's way.

Organizations and Institutions of Reform Judaism

UNION OF AMERICAN HEBREW CONGREGATIONS (UAHC)

838 Fifth Avenue
New York, New York 10021
212-249-0100

REGIONAL OFFICES

Canadian Council
534 Lawrence Avenue West, Suite 210
Toronto, Ontario, Canada M6A 1A2
416-787-9838

Great Lakes Council/Chicago Federation
100 West Monroe Street, Room 312
Chicago, Illinois 60603
312-782-1477

Mid-Atlantic Council
2027 Massachusetts Avenue, N.W.
Washington, D.C. 20036
202-232-4242

Midwest Council
10425 Old Olive Street Road
Suite 205
St. Louis, Missouri 63141
314-997-7566

New Jersey-West Hudson Valley Council
One Kalisa Way
Suite 108
Paramus, New Jersey 07652
201-599-0080

New York Federation of Reform Synagogues
838 Fifth Avenue
New York, New York 10021
212-249-0100

Northeast Council
1330 Beacon Street
Suite 355
Brookline, Massachusetts 02146
617-277-1655

Northeast Lakes Council/Detroit Federation
25550 Chagrin Boulevard
Suite 108
Beachwood, Ohio 44122
216-831-6722

Northern California Council/
Pacific Northwest Council
703 Market Street
Suite 1300
San Francisco, California 94103
415-392-7080

Pacific Southwest Council
6300 Wilshire Boulevard
Suite 1475
Los Angeles, California 90048
213-653-9962

Pennsylvania Council/Philadelphia Federation
2111 Architects Building
117 South 17th Street
Philadelphia, Pennsylvania 19103
215-563-8183

Southeast Council/South Florida Federation
Doral Executive Office Park
3785 N.W., 82nd Avenue
Suite 210
Miami, Florida 33166
305-592-4792

Southwest Council
13777 North Central Expressway
Suite 411
Dallas, Texas 75243
214-699-0656

WORLD UNION FOR PROGRESSIVE JUDAISM (WUPJ)

838 Fifth Avenue
New York, New York 10021
212-249-0100

CAMP INSTITUTES

Kutz Camp Institute
Bowen Road
Box 443
Warwick, New York 10990
914-986-1174

Eisner Camp Institute
Brookside Road
Great Barrington, Massachusetts 01230
413-528-1652

Harlam Camp Institute
R.D. #1
Kunkletown, Pennsylvania 18058
717-629-1390

117 South 17th Street
Philadelphia, PA 19103
215-563-8726/8183

Coleman Camp Institute
Route #3
Cleveland, Georgia 30528
404-865-4111/3521

3785 NW 82nd Avenue
Suite 210
Miami, Florida 33166
305-592-4792

Olin-Sang-Ruby Camp Institute
600 Lac La Belle Drive
Oconomowoc, Wisconsin 53066
414-567-6277

100 West Monroe Street
Chicago, Illinois 60603
312-782-1477

Myron S. Goldman Camp Institute
9349 Moore Road
Zionsville, Indiana 46077
317-873-3361

Jacobs Camp Institute
Box 16528
Jackson, Mississippi 39236-0528
601-362-6357

Box C
Utica, Missisippi 39175
601-885-6042

Greene Family Camp
Bruceville, Texas 76630
817-859-5411

Swig Camp Institute
24500 Big Basin Way
Saratoga, California 95070
408-867-3469

703 Martin Street
Suite 1300
San Francisco, California 94103
415-392-7080

HEBREW UNION COLLEGE-JEWISH INSTITUTE OF RELIGION

3101 Clifton Avenue
Cincinnati, Ohio 45220
513-221-1875

The Brookdale Center
One West 4th Street
New York, New York 10012
212-674-5300

3077 University Mall
Los Angeles, CA 90007
213-749-3424

12 King David Street
Jerusalem, Israel
02 2 32 444

CENTRAL CONFERENCE OF AMERICAN RABBIS (CCAR)

21 East 40th Street
New York, New York 10016
212-684-4990

NATIONAL ASSOCIATION OF TEMPLE EDUCATORS (NATE)
707 Summerly Drive
Nashville, Tennessee 32709
615-352-0322

KADIMA

534 Lawrence Avenue West
Suite 210
Toronto, Ontario, Canada M6A 1A2
416-787-9838

The following organizations have offices at the UAHC (838 Fifth Ave., New York, 10021)

National Federation of Temple Sisterhoods (NFTS)

North American Federation of Temple Youth (NFTY)

National Association of Temple
Administrators (NATA)

American Conference of Cantors (ACC)

Association of Reform Zionists of America (ARZA)

National Federation of Temple Brotherhoods (NFTB)/
Jewish Chataqua Society

Bibliography

The following sources, listed alphabetically, should be of enormous help to a teacher who wishes in-depth information on the various subjects covered in the text. Two sources, the *Jewish Encyclopedia* (New York: Funk and Wagnalls Company, 1905) and the *Encyclopedia Judaica* (Keter Publishing House, Ltd., 1971) can be invaluable in providing quick refreshers and starting points for further investigation. (A key article in the *JE* is by Emil G. Hirsch and David Philipson. It appears in Volume X on pages 347–359 and is entitled "Reform Judaism from the Point of View of the Reform Jew." The entry on "Reform Judaism" in the *EJ*— Volume XIV, pages 23–28—is also very worthwhile.)

Bial, Morrison David. *Liberal Judaism at Home—The Practices of Modern Reform Judaism.* New York: Union of American Hebrew Congregations (UAHC), 1971.

Blau, Joseph L. *Modern Varieties of Judaism.* New York: Columbia University Press, 1966.

Borowitz, Eugene B. *Reform Judaism Today* (plus *A Teacher's Guide,* prepared by Joel Soffin, 1979). New York: Behrman House, Inc., 1978.

Chazan, Robert and Raphael, Marc Lee. *Modern Jewish History: A Source Reader.* New York: Schocken, 1974.

Freehof, Solomon B. *Reform Jewish Practice and Its Rabbinic Background.* New York: KTAV Publishing House, Inc., 1976.

Hertzberg, Arthur. *The French Enlightenment and the Jews.* New York, London and Philadelphia: published jointly by Columbia University Press and the Jewish Publication Society, 1968.

Keeping Posted. Issues of the magazine published by the UAHC and the various mini-courses in subjects of Jewish interest designed for high school and adult use. A catalogue is available (e.g., "What is Reform?" *KP* Vol. XXIV, No. 1, September 1978).

Langer, Michael. *A Reform Zionist Perspective—Judaism and Community in the Modern Age.* New York: UAHC, 1977.

Martin, Bernard (ed). *Contemporary Reform Jewish Thought.* Chicago: CCAR and Quadrangle Books, 1968.

Mendes-Flohr, Paul R. and Reinharz, Jehuda. *The Jew in the Modern World—A Documentary History.* New York and London: Oxford University Press, 1980.

Meyer, Michael A. *The Origins of the Modern Jew—Jewish Identity and European Culture in Germany, 1749–1824.* Detroit: Wayne State University Press, 1967.

Philipson, David. *The Reform Movement in Judaism* (revised edition). New York: KTAV Publishing House, Inc., 1967.

Plaut, W. Gunther. *A Shabbat Manual*. New York: KTAV, 1971.

   —*The Growth of Reform Judaism*. New York: World Union for Progressive Judaism, Ltd. (WUPJ), 1965.

   —*The Rise of Reform Judaism*. New York: WUPJ, 1963.

Polish, David. *Renew Our Days—The Zionist Issue in Reform Judaism*. Jerusalem: World Zionist Organization and WUPJ, 1976.

Raphael, Marc Lee. *Profiles in American Judaism—The Reform, Conservative, Orthodox and Reconstructionist Traditions in Historical Perspective*. San Francisco: Harper and Row, 1984.

Schauss, Hayyim. *The Jewish Festivals*. New York: UAHC, 1969.

   —*The Lifetime of a Jew Throughout the Ages of Jewish History*. UAHC, 1950.

Schwartzman, Sylvan D. *Reform Judaism Then and Now*. New York: UAHC, 1971.

FOR LITURGICAL REFERENCE:

A Passover Haggadah—The New Union Haggadah prepared by the Central Conference of American Rabbis. New York: Grossman Publishers, a division of The Viking Press, 1974.

Gates of Mitzvah—A Guide to the Jewish Life Cycle. New York: Central Conference of American Rabbis (CCAR), 1979.

Gates of Prayer—The New Union Prayerbook. New York: CCAR, 1975.

Gates of Repentance—The New Union Prayerbook for the Days of Awe. New York: CCAR, 1978.

Gates of the House—The New Union Home Prayerbook. New York: CCAR, 1977.

Gates of Understanding. New York: UAHC for the CCAR, 1977.

Glossary

ALEINU ("It is incumbent upon us . . ."): One of the most important prayers in the entire prayer book, it was composed at least as early as the third century C.E. It was originally part of the shofar service on Rosh Hashanah, but by the twelfth century, it was already being read at the end of every service (i.e., morning, afternoon and evening, Shabbat and festivals).

ALIYAH ("ascent," "going up"): The term is used for two specific kinds of "going up." It refers to those who visit Israel (*aliyat regel* = pilgrimage) and, more specifically, to people who move to Israel (known as *olim*, those who go on aliyah). In the synagogue, one who has an aliyah is "called up" to read or chant the blessings which precede and follow the Torah portion for that service.

ARAMAIC: An early Semitic language closely related to Hebrew and now using the same alphabet. Parts of the biblical books of Ezra and Daniel are in Aramaic; so are a number of major prayers, including the Kol Nidre on Yom Kippur eve and the kaddish (the prayer which serves as punctuation between sections of the service; it has also become the prayer recited by mourners and in remembrance of those who have died). Much of the Talmud and the works of Jewish mysticism are also in Aramaic.

CONFIRMATION: A group ceremony for Jewish youth, usually at the end of tenth grade, marking the conclusion of formal Jewish studies and serving as a public affirmation that they accept their obligations as Jewish adults.

CONSERVATIVE JUDAISM: A modern movement in Judaism which developed in Western Europe in the middle of the nineteenth century and flourished in this country from the early twentieth century. Like Reform Judaism, it is dedicated to creating a Jewish way of life for modern Jews. Unlike Reform, it makes the observance of mitzvot* an obligation, not a matter of personal choice—it "conserves" traditional Judaism. Most Conservative congregations therefore are far more traditional in their ritual practices than are most Reform congregations. Because individual congregations can exercise their own options, within certain limits, strange anomalies exist in the Conservative movement. For instance, the Conservative movement now ordains women as rabbis. Yet in some Conservative congregations, women are not allowed to be called for the Torah for an aliyah* and are not counted in a minyan (a religious quorum—by tradition, ten men).

CONVERT: Someone who was not born to Jewish parents who chooses to become a Jew. Conversion involves the study of Judaism (basic religious practices, holidays and customs, Jewish history, Hebrew, etc.) plus, according to halakhah (Jewish religious law), mikveh and (for male converts) ritual circumcision. Reform Judaism does not require mikveh or circumcision for conversion.

EMANCIPATION: The legalization of the Jews as full citizens, with privileges and responsibilities equal to those of all other citizens. The Emancipation followed the French

Revolution (1789) and was part of the extension of equal rights and citizenship to everyone, first in France and later in other parts of Europe. The Emancipation opened up unimagined new possibilities for Jews and also, for the first time in history, made participation in the Jewish community voluntary. Reform Judaism, neo-Orthodoxy and, later, Conservative Judaism were all responses to the challenges of freedom, all ways to let Jews be modern and at the same time stay Jewish.

FEDERATION/UJA: The Jewish communities of North America are organized geographically, across religious and all other lines, into Federations which serve as the central address for each community or group of communities. The Federation administers and funds Jewish social service agencies (senior citizen housing, family service, counseling, day care centers, etc.), funds local Jewish community centers (YM-YMHAs), and supports day schools and other Jewish educational institutions, etc. The Community Relations Council of each Federation deals with the Jewish community's relations with the non-Jewish community. Committees of the Federation also coordinate community responses to the needs of world Jewry. The United Jewish Appeal raises the funds each Federation uses for its own local needs as well as the large portion of the funds it sends to support national Jewish agencies, for Israel and to help disadvantaged and endangered Jews all around the world.

GHETTO: The ghetto was a walled-in section of a city or town where all of the Jews were required to live. The first "official" walled ghetto was in Venice, Italy in 1516, but Jews had been segregated from Christians by the Third Lateran Council of the Church in 1179; a ghetto was established for Jews in London in 1276 (and lasted until the Jews were expelled from England in 1290); from 1294 the Jews of France were required to live apart from the rest of the population; and in 1791, the Jews of Russia were confined to the territory known as the Pale of Settlement. Enforced ghettoization kept many Jews unaware of cultural, social and scientific developments in the larger world. In the ghetto, Jewish life was ruled by Jewish law. Many ghetto Jews never learned or knew only a few words in the language of the country in which they lived; their native language and normal language of communication was *Yiddish* or one of the other Jewish languages. The Emancipation* broke down the ghetto walls in Western Europe.

HASIDISM: An anti-intellectual, religious/mystical movement in Judaism begun in Eastern Europe in the eighteenth century by Israel Ben Eliezer, known as the Baal Shem Tov (Master of the Good Name). Hasidism sought, through Judaism, to compensate Jews for the grinding poverty in which they were submerged. It substituted emotion for study, encouraging Jews to approach Judaism with singing, dancing and fervor. Many stories tell of miracles performed by Hasidic masters, chief among them being the Baal Shem Tov himself.

HAVDALAH ("separation"): The short religious ceremony marking the conclusion of Shabbat and its separation from the new week now beginning. The blessings also note that havdalah separates "light from darkness," the "holy from the profane" and (in traditional prayer books) "Israel from the other nations." Blessings are made over a cup of wine (kiddush), a braided candle and a spice box. There is also a havdalah ceremony at the end of Yom Kippur, the Sabbath of Sabbaths.

HEVRA (OT): Literally, a group of friends, or fellowship; by extension, a volunteer group or society, as in the *hevra kaddisha*, the burial society which traditionally performed all of the necessary functions that are today often handled by funeral homes.

HUPPAH: The canopy held during a Jewish wedding ceremony over the heads of bride and groom. In ancient Israel, a tree was planted at the birth of each baby and it became traditional to use boughs cut from those trees for the huppah. The term is by extension also applied to the actual wedding ceremony itself.

INTERMARRIAGE: The marriage between two people of different religions; specifically, between a Jew and someone who is not Jewish. Intermarriage is also sometimes referred to as mixed marriage. Once the non-Jewish partner has converted to Judaism that person is considered to be a Jew and the marriage is *not* an intermarriage. (Sociologists, however, do call this last category "intermarriage," differentiating it from a "mixed marriage"—for them a marriage between two people of different religions.)

KASHRUT: The ritually proper dietary laws of traditional Judaism. These include not mixing meat products with dairy, not eating pork in any form, or any shellfish, predators or scavengers. Reform Judaism made kashrut, like other mitzvot*, not binding but rather a matter of informed individual choice. Some Reform Jews and some Reform congregations keep kosher; most today do not.

KIBBUTZ YAHEL: The first kibbutz (collective settlement in Israel) founded by the Reform movement, it is also the first religious non-Orthodox kibbutz. It is located deep in the Negev, not far from Eilat. The members of the kibbutz take their Reform Judaism very seriously and make informed decisions as a group about such matters as work permitted on Shabbat, kashrut in public eating places, and all the other matters of Jewish religious life that Reform Jews are free to choose for themselves.

KIPPAH (yarmulke): The skullcap worn at all times by observant Jewish males and by all traditional and many Reform Jews during religious services and at meals. Today some women, particularly in liberal congregations, have also chosen to wear a kippah during worship. In the East, it was a sign of respect to keep one's head covered; in the West, a man would remove his hat in the presence of those he wished to respect. The hats on/hats off issue is thus a matter of tradition vs. conflicting and shifting understandings of proper decorum.

LITERARY PROPHETS: The biblical prophets whose writings are collected in the books bearing their names (Isaiah, Jeremiah, Ezekiel and the twelve "minor" prophets, including Amos, Hosea, Micah, etc.). The other prophets, like Elijah, are sometimes called the "oral" (as opposed to "literary") prophets because their prophecies and the stories about them appear in such books as Samuel and Kings.

MAHZOR ("cyclical"): The festival prayer book, so called because the book follows the cycle of the Jewish festival calendar. The daily and Shabbat prayer book is known in Hebrew as the *siddur*, which means "order."

MESSIAH (lit., "anointed"): The king appointed by God to rule over Israel and all the world at the "end of days," ushering in a time of peace and happiness for everyone. According to traditional belief, at that time the entire Jewish people would be resurrected and gathered from the four corners of the Exile to be reestablished in its ancient land, Israel. Reform Judaism rejected the notion of a personal messiah and a belief in the physical return of all Jews, living or dead, to Israel, and turned instead to the belief in a time when all human beings would cease to do evil and humankind would thus be redeemed, creating the "kingdom of God."

MIDRASH ("investigation" or "inquiry"): The search for meanings that go beyond the literal interpretation of the Bible, for purposes of understanding the spirit of the text and deriving from it ways of applying biblical laws to life. The Midrash is a work of scholarly creativity that consists of moral teachings, fanciful stories and parables—in short, as Leopold Zunz proved, a compendium of popular sermons. Part of the Midrash, *Midrash Halakhah*, is legalistic; the rest, *Midrash Aggadah*, contains ethical teachings, theology and folklore.

MITZVAH (VOT): Technically, a mitzvah is a divine commandment. According to Jewish tradition, the Torah enumerates 613 positive and negative commandments. Because the Torah does not provide a list, however, the specific nature of the 613 is not constant from one source to another. The term has also come to mean a "good deed."

MUSAF: The "additional" service recited in traditional congregations on the mornings of Shabbat and festivals and on the first day of each new month to match the additional animal sacrifice that took place on those days in the Temple in Jerusalem. Reform Judaism deleted this repetition from the prayer book.

MYSTICISM: Known in Hebrew as kabbalah, the "received" tradition, a belief in an "inner" or "higher" reality than is normally perceived. Mysticism is an attempt to "know" God and comprehend God's majesty. For Jewish mystics, every human act is filled with great spiritual significance and provides an opportunity to draw closer to God. Kabbalah is a very complex subject that defies simple glossary definition. It is also one that is of increasing interest to young people because of the rise of fascination with non-rational approaches to religion and to life.

ORTHODOX JUDAISM: The branch of Judaism that accepts Jewish religious law, halakhah, as binding. Because Orthodox Judaism is an orthodoxy, its adherents are convinced they are right and many are therefore very intolerant of the other movements in Judaism and may be reluctant to deal with non-Orthodox Jews. The most serious divisions occur in the manner of conversion to Judaism (and the patrilineal descent issue) and in the matter of religious divorce. Many people—in every movement in Judaism—who are concerned about the Jewish community fear that the divisions within Judaism are becoming frighteningly wide and they worry for the future of the Jewish people. In Israel today, the Orthodox rabbinate exerts control over the country's religious life and fights against any attempts by liberal Judaism to appeal to Israelis.

PIYYUTIM: Liturgical poems, composed from around the fifth century until the eighteenth century. Many thousands of such poems have been catalogued. They were generally incorporated into the worship services to supplement existing prayers. One of the earliest "reforms" of the early Reform movement was the removal of most of these poems from the Reform liturgy.

RABBI(S) ("my teacher" or "my master"): The ordained scholars and sages whose interpretations of the Bible and Oral Law shaped Judaism from the first centuries of the Common Era. (In Babylonia, the term Rav was substituted for Rabbi.) In modern times, rabbis are the professional teachers, preachers and spiritual leaders of congregations and the Jewish community as a whole.

SAGES: The teachers and scholars of the Jewish people during the period of the Talmud. See Rabbis.

SCIENTIFIC METHOD OF JUDAISM (WISSENSCHAFT DES JUDENTUMS): A nineteenth century movement for the study of Jewish history, literature and religious ideas by the methods of modern university scholarship (hence, the term "scientific"). There had been no systematic study of Judaism prior to that time. Wissenschaft des Judentums originated in Germany, was a result of opportunities made available by the Emancipation and served the needs of the developing Reform movement very well. The work of Wissenschaft laid the groundwork for the kind of "Jewish studies" we know in the twentieth century.

TEFILLAH ("*the* prayer"), also known as amidah (the "standing" prayer): The central prayer of every Jewish worship service, for which all worshipers traditionally stand. (The *Union Prayer Book* did not direct worshipers to stand for this prayer, and the choice became a matter of congregational preference. *Gates of Prayer* directs worshipers to stand for the amidah.) On weekdays, it consists of 19 (originally 18) blessings and petitions. On Shabbat, only the seven *berakhot* (blessings) that thank and praise God (rather than those that ask God to "do" things) are included. The tefillah probably dates to a time as early as the last centuries of the Second Temple. The *avot* and *gevurot* are the two opening benedictions of the tefillah. It is appropriate to add personal prayers and petitions during the silent recitation of the amidah. The word *tefillah* also simply means "prayer" and the Hebrew term for worship services is *tefillot*.

TZEDAKAH (literally, "righteousness" or "justice"): The "righteous acts" which, in Jewish tradition, have come to include compassionate philanthropic activity on behalf of the needy and disadvantaged—particularly, but not exclusively, within the Jewish community. Taking financial responsibility for the well-being of the Jewish community means doing what is right. Tzedakah is *not* charity—to be given because it "feels good" or because one is moved by the particular plight of a group or individual. Such contributions are, of course, legitimate and sometimes desirable. But tzedakah is much more: it is an *obligation* incumbent upon all Jews. The United Jewish Appeal is the major collector and disburser for tzedakah for the American Jewish community.

YIDDISH: A language constructed mostly of medieval German and Hebrew, with some Russian and Slavic words, written in Hebrew characters. Hebrew was considered the holy language (*lashon ha-kodesh*) and unsuitable for daily use; Yiddish served for normal communication. It was the native language of most Jews in Central and Eastern Europe. The vast majority of Yiddish speakers were murdered during the Holocaust and relatively few people know how to speak, read or write Yiddish today. Other Jewish languages include Judezmo (Ladino), Judeo-Arabic, Judeo-Persian, Judeo-Tat and Maghrebi, Judeo-Greek, Judeo-Provencal and Jude-Italian.